YOU CAN'T WALLPAPER MY IGLOO

⌘

Tales of Living and Teaching in the Alaskan Wilderness

Written and Illustrated

BY

KATHERINE NORBERG

KATHERINE NORBERG

ISBN-13 978-1490306964

ISBN-10 149030696X

Map of Alaska showing the locations
of places mentioned in this account.

⌘ Dedication ⌘

For my husband, Bob, who promised that my life would not be ordinary. A promise well kept.

Alaska or Bust!

Dawson Creek, Canada: Milepost 0 of the ALCAN
June 1969

The Last Frontier - June 1969

v

CONTENTS

PART I
TOGIAK VILLAGE

PART II

TANANA AND THE YUKON RIVER

PART III
HOMER AT LAND'S END

FORWARD

⌘

How It All Started

I knew it would be an unconventional alliance when I decided to marry Bob. Actually, that's precisely what attracted me to the idea. I knew that our life together would not fit any stereotype; there would be no little house surrounded by a white picket fence for me. What I didn't know was just how far off the beaten track our journey through life would take us, and, although I wasn't dragged off kicking and screaming, I did protest once in a while. I guess it wasn't with enough conviction however, because I always ended up going along with whatever oddity was at hand.

At any rate, when I look back on all the ups and downs, there really isn't much I regret doing. I guess that's a positive mark in anybody's book.

PART I

⌘

TOGIAK VILLAGE

TOGIAK, ALASKA

Fish Cache - Togiak - Fall 1969

Bob gets help chopping wood for the steam bath.

3

Moravian cemetery - Togiak - Fall 1969

Adopted sled dog on icy Togiak Bay - Spring 1970

❦ CHAPTER 1 ❧

SETTING THE STAGE

The wind's cold breath rustled the new spears of tundra grass, whispering, perhaps, of the time when two people from far away would come to this place. Perhaps it knew that the grasses, changed in form, would leave with those people.

A small lemming, her nose in perpetual motion, scratched her way through the tangled undergrowth of grasses to the edge of the low cliff from where she could observe the silent bay below. Ever watchful, she kept a wary eye out for any moving shadow, knowing death could come from above in the form of the sweeping talons of the bald eagle.

So she didn't plan to stay long. As she stood on her hind legs, whiskers twitching with a life all their own, she wasn't aware that she, too, would come to know the people.

And the people would come to know the eagle.

A few miles away, lying on his belly on a rocky beach, a baby seal waited for his mother to come back from her morning swim in the freezing waters of the bay. Hungry, he couldn't be bothered with a thought of the distant future when he, too, would keep his date with the destiny he shared with the people.

Although it was early, this June morning, the arctic sun had been up for a long while, indeed, almost the entire night. It bathed everything in a bright clear light but gave very little warmth. Today would follow closely the pattern of yesterday, the day before, and the day before that.

And the wind would keep on whispering.

*   *   *

Today would be different. Hardly a breath stirred the air on this day that my name would change forever—unusual for a Massachusetts morning by the sea, and lucky. Plans for an outside wedding reception would have suffered had it rained.

As I contemplated the view of the immaculately tended lawn from the bedroom window, my thoughts didn't stray far from the event scheduled for the next few hours.

It was a very small, conventional, and beautiful wedding. Everything was as it should be, normal and without surprises. However, our friends and relations did think it a little strange that Bob and I would immediately make the thousand-mile trip from the very civilized state of Massachusetts to begin our married life in the wilds of New Mexico.

"They have snakes and scorpions, and the people... well... they're odd. They talk funny and chew tobacco. There won't be anybody to hang your drapes or to landscape the yard. What kind of strange existence is that going to be? How are you going to cope?"

We tried to allay some well-intentioned misgivings by offering that at least we did have a small but normal house waiting for us. Bob had bought it during his stay there the year before. The yard however, could pose a problem or two; it was mainly dry dirt and goat-heads, those little burrs with very sharp, painful thorns. They stuck to everything and ended up on your carpet, lying in wait for you to walk by in bare feet.

"Strange" was a relative term because trying new things and places seemed quite normal to us. I had spent my childhood in Europe, Bob was from Chicago, we attended college in Iowa, we married in Massachusetts, and now we were heading for the Wild West.

It seemed like a natural progression.

Once firmly established among the tumbleweed and the sand washes, we began our married life with all the trappings of normalcy. We both had positions teaching in the local junior high school located across our back yard, we shopped in the local market and we did try valiantly to grow grass in our front yard. When we weren't teaching, we would be riding motorcycles, hunting, visiting local points of interest or enjoying a favorite pastime getting lost out in the desert in our four-wheel drive Landcruiser, ostensibly looking for buried Indian pottery. We were never lost for very long, but we thought we were being brazenly adventurous on our outings.

After a while, I guess life began to feel very tame because before long, the wanderlust bug bit again.

Having seen an ad for interviews in Albuquerque for teaching positions in Alaska, we decided to try our luck. As it turned out, the interviewers thought we would fit the bill nicely, and gave us unspecified positions.

Later we realized that a pulse, a normal body temperature, and an absence of criminal record were probably the main criteria for hiring.

I mentioned the word "unspecified" because it was not revealed to us where, in the millions of acres that make up the forty-ninth state, we would be "stationed." We were just guaranteed positions of some kind, somewhere. It was just a job after all.

ð CHAPTER 2 ð

NORTHWARD HO! (Ho, ho, ho.)

It didn't take too long to pack all our belongings into the car and trailer. The only furniture we planned on keeping was our pride and joy: the bedroom set. We were hoping that Bob's folks in Chicago wouldn't mind storing it for a while during our stay up North. Actually, I don't think they would've minded storing us for a while, if only to protect us from ourselves.

We left our newfound New Mexico friends in the settling dust of the driveway. I'm almost certain that they were shaking their heads in mild disbelief, but I could be wrong...

We drove all night, impatient to reach Bob's folks and to get going on our "real trip." I remember pulling off to the side of the road for a little sleep because the tar spots on the road were getting up and jumping at me through the windshield.

* * *

The stay at my in-laws is just a blur in my memory. We dropped off everything we thought we could do without, and some we couldn't, and packed everything else in and on the Landcruiser. We took extra care to stuff the luggage rack as full as possible so that we would have a few more inches of room inside the car. Then we tied it snugly to the fiberglass top of the Toyota. We said our tearful good-byes and headed off into the sunrise. I noticed that Bob's parents were shaking their heads much in the same way our friends back in New Mexico had. Apparently everyone knew something we didn't.

Ignorance is bliss.

For a while, we rode in silence, each preoccupied with private thoughts. Then...

"What was that?"

Something had made a weird noise. We both looked at each other and then looked at the side mirrors.

Realization didn't take long to set in. Several hundred yards down the road our brand new luggage rack had bounced off the flexible fiberglass roof of the jeep. Everything we had so carefully stuffed into the rack now lay in the road for several hundred yards, making it look as though the Beverly Hillbillies had gone by.

We spent the next hour cramming everything into the already filled-to-bursting back of the car. We had to leave the rack by the side of the road in some insurance company's dumpster for posterity.

That was the first time I realized what an interesting and extensive vocabulary my husband had.

After a beginning so auspicious, we figured things could only improve. They did, until we came to a sudden stop at the next traffic light.

Who could have guessed that a stop from twenty-five miles an hour can propel the entire contents of a jeep-type vehicle into the front seat? We found out quickly that it can. By the end of the journey we had become expert car-packers, but it took about seventeen stops to master that science.

After endless mid-west landscape, we approached the Canadian border at International Falls, Minnesota. And it wasn't without some trepidation that we stopped at the checkpoint. This was because we had Bob's entire arsenal of rifles, (then elephant, and now moose) and bow and arrows, (then paper target, and now arctic varmint) on board, and we knew something special would have to be done to them for legal passage through Canada. I think that Bob was harboring visions of the big, mean, square-jawed Dudley Doright Mounties stripping him of his collection.

No such thing, however.

The rifles were simply put into a large plastic container and sealed for passage through Canada. The Mounties would only get mean if the seal was broken at the other end of the trans-Canadian leg of our journey, before the checkpoint.

No big problem there ... unless something attacked us and we had to open the bag in an emergency.

On second thought however, we figured we'd rather take our chances with the unknown than with the RCMP.

We tried to put in as much mileage as possible each day, but on the treacherous gravel of the Alaska Canadian Highway (aka the ALCAN), we barely managed four hundred miles per ten-hour driving day.

We dodged flying gravel and potholes and probably aged our jeep prematurely for the 1500 miles of the worst road and the best scenery we had ever seen. We saw our first moose, bear, mountain goat and caribou. The road was lined with a profusion of wildflowers that looked deceptively frail as they nodded their delicate heads in the breeze. They were probably the toughest plants in the plant kingdom, being able to withstand all sorts of weather even in one season. The twenty-four hour sun helped their vigorous growth.

We saw lakes of the clearest blue-green, undergrowth the most tangled, and outhouses the most antique with accompanying graffiti, the most quaint. We came to the conclusion that bathroom humor is sort of international unless the same mysterious tourist was preceding us each place we stopped.

Anyway, it gave us something to talk about as we gritted our teeth through the next hundred miles of...well...grit. Our windshield was beginning to look like we had traversed the entire eastern front line of the German army during the Second World War.

Bumping along the Alaska-Canada Highway.

We would make bets as to which jagged lines would link which nicks across our line of vision first. A spider would have felt very much at home with this abstract pattern, and I'm sure that the frown lines we formed from squinting through the window have graced our foreheads ever since.

* * *

"What time is it?"

For people who are used to the daylight and darkness determining their daily habits such as getting up and going to bed, living in the higher latitudes can prove to be somewhat disconcerting.

13

If you are exposed to it in the summer months, you can wait until much later than the cows coming home before seeing dusk fall. In fact, if the cows are waiting for it in order to come home, you can forget the whole thing. The sun seems to hang indefinitely in the depths of blue sky as if the normal daily cycle has been suspended. Ten P.M. looks like three in the afternoon.

By the time we reached the great unknowns of the Yukon province, we had to rely on our stomachs and eyelids to know what daily habit we were supposed to be practicing.

"Why not use a watch?" one might ask quite sensibly.

Our watches were great for telling us Central Standard Time in the good ole' USA, but there were no signposts to tell us when we had just crossed a time zone. In fact, there were very few signposts that told us anything except how many miles we'd been since Dawson Creek at the beginning of the ALCAN. We did know the time to the exact minute in Chicago, which was the last place we had paid attention to our watches, or even to time altogether. We were much more interested in just being aware of what day it was. The time of day seemed somehow particularly irrelevant.

After having admired the beauty of numerous places that had been up to this point only names in the "Milepost" (the bible used for travel in northwest Canada and Alaska), we lingered only long enough to pay hurried homage to places which were mentioned, or to get a few hours of sleep in any establishment that would have us.

It was a real stretch of the imagination to accept the term "Inn" for some of the housing that tried to pass for one.

One place that did hold our interest, however, was on the border between British Columbia and the Yukon Territory. Liard Hot Springs provided a welcome interlude for the weary traveler.

Stripping down to our bathing suits that we had packed in the upper quadrant of our mound of stuff, we walked down a narrow boardwalk, (punching out mosquitoes that were being quite territorial), leading us to pools of surprisingly clear water ranging in temperature from warmish to scalding. We stayed in as long as we could stand it, trying to see who could move nearer and nearer to the source of the hot springs and withstand the most pain.

The contest was a standoff.

Looking like a pair of oversized but thoroughly wrinkled lobsters, we oozed our way back to the car to dry off and get our clothes back on. We found a little lodge nearby that had a few rooms and a small cafe. After a good meal, it took us about five minutes to get from our door to the bed and fall asleep. That night was probably the most restful one we had the whole trip.

We knew, at the 1400 milepost, that the border to Alaska was somewhere ahead within the next few dusty miles. Every once in a while, between gravel bullets, we'd catch sight of one vehicle or another sporting license plates with a standing grizzly on them.

What could be more Alaskan?

15

We couldn't wait to get our own testimony of residence in the "Last Frontier." We had lost track of the days, but figured blearily that we had been inflicting damage upon our vehicle and persons for four or five days. After passing through the Canada-Alaska checkpoint at Beaver with our gun seals intact, we tried to guess at which point we would actually cross into Alaska itself.

"Wait!" There it is!"

Jubilation! To the side of the road we caught sight of a larger-than-usual signpost.

We uncoiled ourselves hurriedly from our cramped quarters, and stumbled closer for a look. Suddenly we knew how Balboa or someone must have felt as he caught site of the Pacific. Here was a signpost replete with everything you've always wanted to know about Alaska's statistics but couldn't be bothered to ask. In addition to the numbers of acres, miles of coastline, and altitudes of mountain ranges, it assured us that there were no snakes in the entire state. We set up our camera to take an historic photograph of our "Arrival."

One of us—the really naïve one—sighed dreamily,

"Well, it can't be far to a real motel now. We're back in the states!"

This was only one of the many wrong notions we had for the next few years. "Far" is a completely different concept in a state that spans four time zones, as Alaska did in those days. (It has since been changed to two.) We were salivating at the thought of a good red-blooded American meal at a run-of-the-mill roadside restaurant. In most states you can't avoid them every few miles along the freeways, and they usually seem to run into each other in a blur that you take for granted.

After about fifty slow but steady miles, our spirits picked up as we saw some kind of structure by the roadside ahead. A peeling wooden sign announced: " First ood an   as." (The word "first" was an allusion, we surmised, to this wayside oasis being the first one you came to after crossing the border, and not to the class of it's roadside appeal!)

Still unaccustomed to dealing with the "Alaskan Architectural Look," we decided that this must just be the first in a succession of more roadside rest stops that would prove more attractive. We went on our way, the gas gauge flirting with the empty mark.

How can anyone be so wrong so many times in a row?

It was another fifty miles before we reached any kind of habitation that looked like it could provide the essentials for life: mainly food and drink. At this point, we would have stopped anywhere that even remotely resembled a restaurant.

Our gas tank was as empty as our bellies when we pulled up to the first establishment to pass for such an establishment. I don't remember what we ordered, but starvation makes any dish a gourmet meal.

It would have felt good to take a long nap, but we were anxious to reach Fairbanks before too much more time had elapsed.

We knew we'd have to get set for school and we were anxious to get our bearings before having to tackle classwork. Wiser, we were becoming more wary of things now. Who knew what obstacles were lying in wait on the road ahead? Better gain as much ground as possible just in case.

We also found it hard to believe how warm it was. Weren't we just a few hundred miles from the Arctic Circle? Yet the temperature was in the low nineties and very muggy.

We had already passed Tok, and were within reach of Delta Junction. After that, we'd pass by Fort Richardson Army base, Eielson Air Force base, and then the outskirts of Fairbanks. It took only a few minutes to go around Fairbanks to reach that section of town called College, home of the University of Alaska, our special "boot camp" to prepare us for our new challenge.

❧ CHAPTER 3 ❧

BOOT CAMP

The next few days piled up on one another in rapid succession, as we learned to absorb an onslaught of unexpected events and information.

In order to fulfill our obligation for our new teaching jobs, we were to attend a special project at the University for so-called "bush" teachers: "The Rural Schools Project." It consisted of classes on "culture shock," anthropology, methods for teachers-facing-the-possibility-of-teaching-classes-ranging-from kindergarten-through-eighth-grade-all-in-one-room, and survival in the "great wilderness." We were given food lectures, dress lectures, and behavior lectures with a healthy dose of anthropology.

The food lectures were particularly riveting, especially the ones about "stinky heads." We were told that in many villages, fish were buried underground or dumped into buckets until they had reached a certain critical point at which time they would cause a "slight buzz" if eaten. We were admonished not to eat anything for twenty-four hours before and after partaking in this delicacy—that is, if we wanted to avoid much distress.

I figured I'd just avoid the entire issue. I liked my fish fresh.

We were also told that smoked and dried fish were perfectly safe even if dotted with mold. For those people going north, it was enthusiastically suggested that they try Eskimo ice cream and whale blubber. The recipe for the former had been modernized so that berries were mixed with Crisco shortening rather than the traditional seal oil or blubber. The latter was not unlike thick chewing gum.

They did say you'd eventually get used to the greasy film coating your teeth. Because we were scheduled to go south, the "fish" lectures were more relevant to us than the "blubber" ones.

The anthropology professor liked to dwell on the social and sexual practices of the ancient peoples, the Eskimo, the Aleut, and the various Indian groups. He also continually mentioned "labrets:" studs made of ivory the ancient Eskimos used to wear imbedded just below their lower lip, not unlike the studs worn by the younger generation of today in all the body-piercing rage. But the labrets were much thicker, distending the whole area between the lips and the chin. They were usually decorated with some kind of dye rubbed into etchings.

At this professor's very first lecture, thanks to

my European background, I recognized a Dutch or Flemish accent. I discovered that he was, indeed, of Flemish descent, so, one day, as I happened to be immediately in front of him in the cafeteria line, I decided to surprise him a little. I passed him back a lunch tray saying the Flemish expression for "Here you are." By reflex, he answered, also in Flemish, "Thanks very much." He was about to pick out his main dish when the realization hit him. He hadn't heard his uncommon native tongue in a long time, and here he was, in the middle of the forty-ninth state of a foreign country, population less than most cities, hearing it from some stranger in a cafeteria line. He looked at me, speechless for the first time in a while, I suspected, because he never seemed at a loss for words. I smiled at him and walked off with my chicken-fried something or other, leaving him and his incredulous stare in my wake.

Later, we had occasion to talk of the "old country," Belgium, where he and I had both spent our childhoods. The old cliché, "It's a small world" seemed particularly apt.

One of the unexpected events in our new environment was our first earthquake experience. As we sat in our eighth floor dorm room one day, we became conscious of an ever increasing swaying of the room. It took us a full minute to realize that we were feeling a quake in a building constructed to absorb it. It was the first time that I felt the real and uneasy fear of being totally out of control; a feeling that, I came to find out, it behooved me to get used to.

Just a few years out of college, it was easy to slip back into the "student mode." We lived in a dorm, this time married to our roommate who slept in the other college regulation type bed, eating cafeteria food, and doing our homework (most of the time). We became acquainted with all the other young, naïve couples, who, like us, were about to enter a new and completely unpredictable phase in their lives. Some were about to take on a double whammy because they were beginning married life as well. We were experienced hands at it, having had a whole year of married life under our belts.

It took a while to learn to fall asleep in broad daylight at eleven P.M., to get used to the high temperatures (often ninety to a hundred degrees of muggy heat), to put up with the ever-present smoke of forest fires that seemed to break out every other day or so, and to find a store open on Sundays. In a way, these weeks were a kind of delayed honeymoon for us, as we had never had a formal one. We made several side trips when we could, sightseeing, picnicking, nightclubbing, and generally enjoying a worry-free time.

* * *

At that time, Fairbanks was a city of about twenty-five thousand very mobile people. It was one of those places greatly affected by a boom or bust economy. The population was a mixture of original pioneers, service industry workers, military personnel from the nearby bases, fortune seekers, oil drilling

22

workers and administrators, natives, professors from the University, scientists, and a few regular people like us.

We had heard that there were more PhD's per capita in Alaska than in any other state. Our estimate was that there were certainly more weirdos there than anywhere else. Everybody seemed to be able to do his own thing without constraints of any kind. In fact there was a considerable movement for "Alaskan Independence" whereby the state would secede from the "Lower Forty-eight."

At that time, oil was just beginning to make its impact, and many Alaskan agencies still depended heavily on federal funding. So, secession of any sort would have been a bad move, but we had to admit that it had a romantic ring to it.

As far as nighttime entertainment was concerned, we especially enjoyed a few evenings at "The Malemute Saloon" listening to Robert Service's poetry read in semi-darkness by local talent. The saloon was located a few miles out of Fairbanks in the old mining town of Ester, still boasting gold dredges and gold rush buildings. This saloon was known for its sawdust floor sprinkled with millions of peanut shells dropped by the mesmerized patrons listening to "The Cremation of Sam McGee" and the "Shooting of Dan McGrew."

Downtown Fairbanks, consisting mainly of First through Fourth avenues with their accompanying cross streets, afforded other entertainment. Originally a tent city situated along the banks of the Chena River, it had developed mostly south of it. The only department store was your basic J C Penney's. There was a Sears catalog order store, a few miscellaneous drugstores, and hardware stores, etc.

Each weekend, our light blue Landcruiser could be seen winding its way through the streets of Fairbanks as we scrutinized spots for "good deals" that Bob felt we absolutely needed.

The biggest businesses were probably the Army-Navy surplus stores. We spent many hours there while Bob examined every item. They did have some good long underwear and mitts that we needed, but the necessity of owning thirty-year-old K-rations and a jungle machete still causes occasional argument.

☙ CHAPTER 4 ❧

PREVIEW OF COMING ATTRACTIONS

The mainstay of the university program, or the "do or die" part as we called it, came at a point towards the end of the session. This was the week "in the field" part that involved getting flown to the specific village in which we were going to spend the next nine months of our lives.

We were to be flown to a small southern Eskimo village called Togiak, located on a small bay that seemed to be just about where the Pacific Ocean and the Bering Sea meet. This was to be our home for the year. I guess the idea of the visit was to give the more squeamish souls a last chance to back out if they thought they wouldn't be able to stand the culture shock.

I guess this would be a good place to talk about igloos, since the word Eskimo seems to bring them to mind almost immediately. I cannot put a number on the amount of people who asked us, upon our visits home, if we had lived in one.

Eskimo Igloo

As we were instructed in our anthropology classes, igloos were mainly built as temporary housing when families traveled away from home from one place to another for various reasons such as following game. They were a sort of do-it-yourself-Motel-6 on the road, used decades ago when travel was slow and hunting constant.

Requiring extreme talent to build, their blocks were made completely from scratch and had to fit together perfectly. These blocks of frozen snow, cut out with a special "snow knife" used for the construction, had to have perfect tapering in order to form the spiral necessary for the finished product. Temperatures inside could rise fifty degrees higher than outside by body heat alone. The heat itself would glaciate the interior and provide more stability and insulation. Families could stay several days in this temporary home and could be quite comfortable. There was a small vent for smoke, ice for "window blocks" to let in whatever light was available outside, and a little Eskimo entrance tunnel that acted as a buffer to prevent the wind and snow from entering the living area.

No igloo builder ever needed blueprints to build this little home. The ability to fashion the igloo was passed from parent to child, and it may very well have been almost genetic because, as modern day tests have shown, Eskimo children seem to have above average ability to perform spatial tasks.

It was with great anticipation, coupled with not a little apprehension that we climbed into the plane in Fairbanks, flew to Anchorage and then climbed aboard a Twin Otter ("Twin" signifying two engines) to reach Dillingham.

This fishing town was purported to be the largest town in the Bristol Bay area, so we were again confronted with discrepancy of terms. "Big" is another one of those concepts that is totally relative. In this case it meant one whole department store (about five "departments": hardware, fishing equipment, small engine parts, boots and outdoor wear, and candy), an airport, a harbor, a post office, a school, and a food market. There were a few dozen houses too, scattered about, and a hospital. Actually, I think there were more houses than we thought, hidden in the gullies and woods, and we later found out that there was a hot nightclub down the road a bit. Little did we know that this town would indeed seem "big" to us in a few months.

After a cursory visit in town, we returned to the airport (a grandiose term for a gravel airstrip) to clamber aboard a "Widgeon."

The encyclopedia describes a widgeon as a species of "dipping" duck related to many others including the mallard, that lives in shallow bodies of water dipping its flat bill in the water for underwater delicacies. When it engages in this behavior, only its tail can be seen sticking up in the air.

This description is only a bit more humorous than the appearance of the apparatus that bears its name. If you imagine an airplane needing to be sleek and streamlined in order to benefit by the aerodynamics necessary for flight, you would look with trepidation at the potbellied vehicle squatting on the airstrip. It looked like the wings had been added as an afterthought by the obviously deranged designer who had gotten away with passing it off as an airplane.

As we squeezed ourselves into its belly I noticed a tag on the inside that informed me that it and I were of the same vintage.

How much is that in airplane years, I wondered.

The pilot was at the front doing, I thought, whatever pilots do in flight preparation. It did not reassure me to suddenly notice that he was actually rummaging around in an old tackle box, examining hooks and lures. As if noticing us for the first time, he exclaimed, " Hey, y'all ready to ride? Les go then."

No speeches about seat belts, oxygen masks or refreshments. This was your basic generic flight.

Somehow the term "No frills" didn't come close to an accurate description.

As we rolled down the airstrip I knew my suspicions about this so-called airplane's capabilities were well founded. I guess the manufacturers had never heard of shock absorbers. I felt as though I was being dragged across the world's longest washboard. No wonder we didn't get complimentary beverages. Whatever it was would have made a milkshake look calm.

I looked around for the ubiquitous brown bag but, in its absence, I guessed the rationale behind not providing one was that a passenger would be too preoccupied with fear to let a little queasiness get in the way.

So the bag was totally unnecessary.

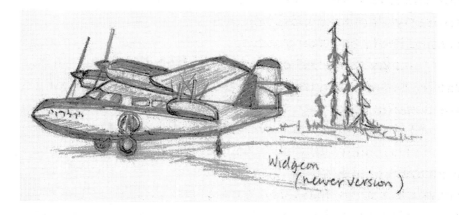

Widgeon
(newer version)

Incredibly, we actually became airborne after an unexpectedly short taxi. The landscape fell away and we were able to see acres of green tundra on rolling hills with the ocean to one side. The pilot did not seem to believe in high altitude flying, playing hide-and-seek with the hilltops.

It was much more fun than I expected.

All of a sudden we banked at an incredible angle and we saw a gray blur streak past our line of vision. The pilot yelled something about landing but I couldn't understand anything else over the noise of the engines. When we came out of the turn, I saw miniature houses and a river, but no landing strip.

It was when we effected a watery landing in the river that I began to appreciate the great versatility of the weird looking Widgeon. It was equipped to land in the water by virtue of its low-slung wide belly, and its little pontoons, and on land, by virtue of its retractable wheels. We stopped only long enough to exchange one mailbag for another, and it was back in the air after a rush of water during the takeoff.

I noticed tiny raindrops on the windshield being forced against it and along the side of the plane. The weather had turned cloudy and dark and the entire countryside had taken on a silver-gray tint. Every once in a while great shafts of sunlight would slice through an opening in the cloud cover, revealing an ocean that was progressively getting much closer to the belly of the plane than before. While I had reasonable, if somewhat shaky confidence in the pilot, it seemed to me that he was now flying by the "braille" method, feeling his way around each hill and valley and swooping down toward the water. I remembered someone commenting on how low pilots would fly around here to get "under" the weather.

In fact, someone said, they had read an article about one such plane that was flying so low it had collided with a boat's mast.

As I looked up at the cliffs to our right, I became an instant believer in the story. We actually had to gain altitude in order to get up over the cliffs to take the last turn to land at our destination.

In a way it was probably a good thing for our state of mind that we didn't get a bird's eye first view of our new home. The sight of two fragile rows of houses hugging a zigzagging airstrip on a flat expanse of sparse tundra might have served to dampen our spirits. Because we had rounded the last bend at such a low altitude, we saw the village from a much closer point and somehow it didn't appear so desolate.

Togiak Village "Freeze up" 1969

By the time we piled out of the 'plane, the weather had worsened, and we became totally soaked as we waited for the janitor to come up with the key to the teacher housing.

*   *   *

The house was normal: a living room, dining area, kitchen, bathroom and two bedrooms. It had electricity and running water. All of these things thanks to the Bureau of Indian Affairs, that had operated the schools in this village before the state had taken over. Federal programs had been more generous in what they provided the schools than the state was able to do. We were going to live a luxurious life compared to the teachers who were stationed in villages where the "honey bucket" was a way of life, and the only running water was in the local river.

One particular tale of the "honey-bucket" remained vivid in my mind. In one of the larger villages, there was actually "honey-bucket brigade service." One of the local people was hired to extract the buckets from below their "sitting" compartments, and empty them each day. One such "removal" occurred at the precise moment it was in use by an unsuspecting teacher. The sudden cold draft of frigid air served too late as warning.

During our week's stay we grew accustomed to the petroleum smell of the water (someone had decided to put the school's fuel tanks right above the water supply), the continuous rainy weather, (it rains or mists more than often in the summer) and the sporadic appearances of giggling little faces at our window and doorstep.

We spent the next few days touring the village to get the feel of our new surroundings. We noted a small plywood building sporting a faded wood sign: Togiak Commercial. This was the only store in the village. It took a few minutes for our eyes to become accustomed to the gloomy interior, and to take mental inventory of its contents.

Among the cases of soda pop and candy, there were some canned goods, some boxed goods, and a few tired heads of lettuce. In a small freezer lay some steaks whose fat had turned yellow with age. If anyone, in spite of the presentation, had had inclination to make a purchase, a look at the price would provide an effective deterrent. You'd have to be pretty desperate to lay out seventeen dollars for a steak that had probably survived several seasons.

We hoped we'd never get that desperate. Our exploration took us to the post office, also a plywood structure, expediently close to the airstrip. These two buildings made up the sum total of the village's commercial buildings.

We moved on to the residential part. The houses were situated in no particular order, some closer together than others. Most of them consisted of two rooms: a living area including a kitchen, and a back area in which the family slept. There was not much in the way of furniture; most items were put on the floor or hung on wall hooks.

We noticed that close to most houses sat a few scraggly sled dogs, a term loosely applied considering their obviously appalling condition. We learned later that many of them were fed their own and human excrement when times were difficult, and most of them never got a chance to pull a sled.

After winding our way through the houses, we came to the cemetery with its many orthodox crosses, testimony to the Russian influence of decades ago. From there we found our way among the drying fish, drying salmon eggs, and drying seal and walrus hides to the meandering slough that formed a natural boundary at the back of the village.

All-Purpose drying rack
Toguik 1969

The tide was out and had left nothing but a shallow ribbon of murky water in the slough bed. The boats were lying on their sides, waiting for high water to right them selves. We walked among the boats and then headed for home in a persistent chilling drizzle.

*   *   *

"Plane! Plane!"

On one of the next gray rainy days, we were awakened by a chorus of children's excited voices, and were surprised by a visit from the superintendent of the area in whose house we were staying. He had arrived in his single engine plane to pack his family's belongings, as they were moving to another village. He flew us to many spots in the network of rivers and streams teeming with running salmon.

It was then that I established myself as the fisherperson of the family. Fishing takes a fine touch, and I guess I was gifted in that area. I caught all eight of the salmon we took home, marking the beginning of many years of my fishing luck.

I don't rub it in too much, but this luck has stood me in good stead, and has provided me with a great deal of verbal ammunition in times of need.

"Mail plane!"

Togiak Village
1969

⤫ CHAPTER 5 ⤬

THE PLUNGE

We decided we could take it. Actually, there were no couples in the entire orientation project that were too horrified at the prospect of living in the "bush" for the winter to give up their positions. Assignments ranged from teaching at one-teacher schools to teaching at regional high schools with a dozen or more teachers. Our assignment rated somewhere in the middle with a grand total of six.

We had met the other couple we would be teaching with, and awarded them mixed reviews. When you're going to be in close exclusive association with someone for at least nine months, it's important that the relationship be positive. I'm one of these people who rely on instinct; the vibes I received were not comforting.

Oh well, just because we had to work with someone didn't mean we'd have to spend all our waking hours in close association. We were still practically newlyweds and would be spending a lot of time on our own, we were sure. The other two teachers who would be teaching with us, and whom we hadn't met, were two single women, members of the Moravian church that had a long history of influence over many of the villages in our area. Just how much influence they had had, we'd soon find out.

Something else momentarily escaped us. It was simple mathematics really. There was a total of six teachers, and two houses at two teachers apiece. That left two teachers without housing. You'd think that this puzzle would sow a seed of mild panic or, at least, a small amount of concern.

We went back to our orientation classes in blissful oblivion however, and never really gave it a thought.

* * *

With the arrival of the month of August came the realization that life, as we knew it, was approaching a new phase. Our classes were wrapping up, and we felt fully armed for what was in store vis-à-vis education, survival, and life in general. We thought we knew everything there was to know about the various cultural and social implications of being in a position of authority while being a minority.

Having been trained as secondary teachers, we had had to learn the intricacies and methods of elementary teaching. We felt we had a handle on that too.

What we didn't have was, A, groceries and supplies to last nine months and, B, money to buy those groceries and supplies.

Our most valuable possession was the jeep we now had to get rid of, and we didn't really know enough about anything to ask the right questions. Up to now we had muddled along so far, so these facts posed no more of a threat than anything else had to this point. To take care of both problems, we sold our jeep (still sporting New Mexico license plates) to someone in Fairbanks for enough money to buy the groceries we needed.

Our fare to Anchorage had been financed by the State Department of Education, so all we had to do was to find a grocery store, and then somehow get the food to our new home.

The big question now was how and where you buy groceries for an entire year. I had always had a tough enough time figuring out what to make for dinner. This threw meal planning into a whole new dimension.

Upon the advice of a veteran bush teacher, we found a wholesale food store whose staff understood the complexities of the matter. We were able to go through the warehouse choosing a case of this and that, institution-sized containers of mustard, ketchup and artichoke hearts, huge boxes of toilet paper etc., ad infinitum. As we didn't think we could stomach an entire case of certain items such as olives and pimientos, we either decided to forgo these delicacies, or to share a case with the other teachers who were also doing their shopping. We had no idea how much toilet paper or toothpaste we'd use, so we'd have to monitor our supplies carefully by taking inventory once in a while. There are some things you just don't want to be caught without when you can't just go to the corner supermarket to get a refill.

All in all, it was a very interesting shopping experience, and the bill was more than a down payment on a car. We even had to borrow from our future associates in order to pay for it all.

Having completed our order, we made arrangements for the groceries to follow us to our station on a different flight. Then we made a drugstore run for the items we did not need in case lots.

At that time, the closest thing Anchorage had to a mall was a supermarket, a drugstore and a movie theatre in one spot. Everything closed early and nothing was open on Sundays. We had to hurry to take care of last minute items and were finally more or less ready to take our leave of civilization.

๛ CHAPTER 6 ๛

THE DISCOMFORTS OF HOME

This time we did get a bird's eye view of the village, but we were psychologically prepared. Undaunted as we were by the vastness of nothingness on the great out door scale, we were nevertheless at least mildly worried about our indoor accommodations.

It had been mentioned, back in civilization, that "some temporary arrangements" would have to be made for our quarters as the permanent housing was yet to be delivered. We realized that since the existing housing had been built with federal funds for the Bureau of Indian Affairs when they had run the school, whatever was to be put in place now by the state would be of different quality. We accepted that without question, just like we accepted the fact that, as new kids on the block, we would be the ones to live in whatever turned up.

It was difficult to keep an open mind however, when the welcoming committee, composed of the janitor and a handful of smiling children, led us to the school building, down the hall and into what appeared to be a primary classroom.

Silly us for thinking that it was a classroom, for over to one side was a double bed of some antiquity with a screen partially hiding it. This was obviously an apartment of some kind. It just looked like a primary classroom with its chalkboard, wall-mounted pencil sharpener, pull-down movie screen, and adjoining toilet.

I guess a sudden involuntary spasm gripped Bob's stomach, as he dashed to the aforementioned bathroom without taking time to turn on the light.

It could have been a costly mistake. One thing that our recent elementary-school-intensive-training-session had not prepared us for was what a long way down it is to a primary school toilet. Bob found out the hard way and almost hurt himself badly.

Well, close to the floor or not, any toilet is better than a "honey bucket," and running water is a true luxury. I kept repeating this to myself as I bent over to wash my hands in the primary sink and wondered at how short little kids must be.

After the initial taking-aback had subsided, we began to assess the good points of living so close to the job. No commuting, no getting up hours before having to be at work, no facing the elements on the way to work (which was no small consideration given the environment), and no bringing the job home. It WAS home. What more could you ask?

Well, for starters, how about a stove? There was nothing on which to cook, no refrigerator, no storage facilities, and a sink about the size of a measuring cup. Somehow, we hadn't bargained for such limited living conditions, but we saw the humor in it and decided to set up whatever we could find in order to better the situation.

Looking back on my just-attained-twenty-one years, I realized how unchallenging and boring regular living conditions had been.

* * *

After a few days of scrounging, we were able to come up with a toaster oven and an electric two-burner stovetop. We used the school refrigerator for storing our prepared powdered milk and a few perishables. It was amazing how you could make do with the minimum if you have to.

We had a bed (actually two steel cots pushed together), and a makeshift system for hanging clothes instead of a closet: a rope strung between a chalkboard hook and a bookshelf. Luckily the windows were equipped with drapes and we pasted some paper to cover the hall door window for privacy. It really wasn't that bad, and anyway, it was temporary—probably only a few days, or possibly a few weeks, at the very most. It doesn't take too much hardiness to stick that brief interlude out.

Two and a half months later, as I pulled a clove-studded Spam out of the toaster oven, and poured powdered milk into the powdered potato buds, I pondered for the millionth time on the many interpretations of "temporary."

True, we were faring admirably. The daily clickety-click of the other teacher's heels, as she came down the hall in the morning, was our secondary alarm system when we decided to snooze a little extra time. If that didn't work, we were encouraged to "rise and shine" by a host of little voices at our door, eager for school to begin.

The utilities all worked perfectly, and we had rearranged our quarters into different little "rooms" by moving the classroom furniture around. We now had a diminutive kitchen, a six by six living room, and a bedroom, all in an almost cozy atmosphere.

Home sweet home is what you make it.

ஓ CHAPTER 7 ௸

IN SEARCH OF ENTERTAINMENT

Increased enrollment dictated that the six of us teachers work in two shifts in the remaining three classrooms. Three of us took the morning shift from seven-thirty to noon, and the other three took the twelve to four-thirty shift. This meant that we had the entire afternoon to ourselves.

Although we spent a sizeable portion of our afternoons making up for our early rising by napping, we did manage to take advantage of the beautiful fall days to walk the tundra and to make some side trips in a rented river skiff.

We had heard that the cannery across the bay,

just about to close for the winter, was showing a movie right after high tide. This could be our last chance for entertainment for nine months.

We didn't plan on missing it.

It couldn't be too hard to pilot the skiff down the slough, through the channel, and across the bay. We knew that, because of the twenty-foot tides, it was imperative to time the trip right, or we'd be stuck halfway across in the mud of the tidal flats. We had noticed that at low tide, we couldn't even see the water and yet at high tide, it came to within a few feet of the school buildings.

There was also the matter of available daylight to consider. Being stuck out in the middle of a tidal flat in the daylight was considerably less frightening than being stuck there when you couldn't see a hand in front of your face. The skiff didn't come with a headlight.

With spirits high at the prospect of facing the unknown, we boarded our vehicle and followed the fleet of boats headed for the cannery. There was a definite feeling of safety in numbers, and we enjoyed the scenery on the five-mile jaunt to the other side. The trip was a snap—nothing to it. Hardly able to suppress our self-satisfied smiles at having reached our destination, we followed the villagers to the cannery.

There was something romantic yet lonely about the place. You expect it to be a hub of activity, a place full of the shouts of workers busy at their posts. Instead, the conveyor belts were stationary, the machinery mute. We could only imagine the activity at the height of the past fishing season. In a way it was almost eerie to make our way in a hushed procession down the walkways to the area where the movie was to be shown.

We passed by the cannery store, a small room to one side of a large warehouse boasting shelves of fare we came to recognize as "bush" staples: candy, pop, and toilet paper. Everyone found a chair facing a makeshift screen and prepared to savor the celluloid bombardment of twentieth century urban American life for an hour and a half. We privately enjoyed the incongruity of the violent city scenes depicted on the screen with the serene landscape outside the window. We spent most of the time observing the audience instead of watching the film we had seen years ago. In fact, we decided to leave before the end, in order to explore the area.

There really wasn't much to see, but we walked quite far down the beach indulging Bob's predilection for junk, one of the by-products of operating a cannery. He had a field day examining all the old machinery, fishing equipment and miscellaneous items piled up all over. I had a hard time convincing him that we didn't need any of it at home.

Before we knew it, twilight was only a few hours off and we hurried back to our skiff. We caught sight of it at the same time that we noticed the absence of the other boats.

Could we have been gone that long?

The hollow feeling we felt in the pit of our stomachs was probably similar to the one you get when the dentist says it'll only hurt a little.

Never mind. The trip over had been without incident, so going the same way back should do the trick. We hurriedly piled in and aimed for the other side of the bay.

Things look so different when you face the other way, and when the sun is at a different angle. We kept the far-off school building as a point of reference, at the same time bearing slightly to the right where we guessed the entrance to the slough should be.

We were surprised by a profusion of seagulls hovering above us, screaming and flapping, as if indignant that we should interrupt their routine. We wondered why there hadn't been any on our way over.

Could the tide have anything to do with it?

We became aware of a constant tinkling of something along the bottom of the boat. It didn't take long to realize that the water was so low that we were lightly dragging the bottom. The sea gulls could dip their beaks to feed right into the muddy bottom.

After a few minutes, our progress was non-existent. The engine shaft, now mired in the oozing mud, became a deficit. There was nothing to do but to use our own power.

One of us pulled and guided from the front, and the other pushed at the other end. We had obviously missed the channel where the deeper water was, so we now aimed directly for the beach in front of the school buildings, still about a quarter of a mile away.

As we approached the beach, the inch of water that had been helping the boat glide relatively smoothly, completely disappeared. Progress had slowed to a very laborious few feet per minute. I noticed with dismay that each step into the mud exerted an extraordinary amount of suction on my hip boots. Then the unthinkable happened. I gave a powerful tug to release my leg from the mud's grip and managed only to extricate my foot from the boot. The inertia of my effort landed me completely in the mud, minus my boot.

Seriously questioning the sanity of anything I had done in the past year, I looked to Bob for help only to find him convulsed with laughter, grappling with our camera.

Adding insult to injury was definitely an art with him.

I glowered, hoping that there wasn't enough light left for the photographic process.

There is justice, however. The action of stopping and standing in the same spot for a minute had served to root him in the mud had just as firmly as I was. Camera hurriedly abandoned, Bob pulled himself out by grabbing the side of the boat, but he couldn't get over to help me. All he could do was to push the boat over so that I could use it to pull myself out.

Desperation can make one accomplish great feats. That's the only way I can explain our not drowning later as the tide came up at two o'clock in the morning. I managed to right myself, retrieve my disappearing hip boot, and hang over the back of the boat while pushing it, inches at a time, until we finally made it to the hard sand of the beach.

Stuck in the mud...
Joyiak 1969

Now we knew why people kiss the ground when they're grateful to have arrived on some shore somewhere. We were tempted, but too exhausted. I gave it a token mental effort.

We spent the next several days scraping and washing mud. Some people asked why we had chosen to come home the hard way. To this day, I don't have a dignified answer.

* * *

After that, realizing that mud baths were overrated, we chose more conservative expeditions. In the mild warmth of the last autumn days, we took our shotguns and walked out in the tundra to get some ducks for dinner. It was just an excuse to go somewhere, because most of the outings found us lying by one of the thousands of land-locked tundra lakes, gazing at the sky and waving lazily at the ducks as they flew by. Someone had said that the ducks tasted so much like fish they weren't worth the time it took to pluck them anyway.

On one such laid-back afternoon, we kept hearing a funny snorting noise as we lay there.

The ever-present threat of bears kept me on the alert. I looked around for the source of the noise.

In the middle of the little lake, floating on its back, an otter enjoyed the late afternoon sun as he played with something on his chest.

We watched him until it was too dark to see him anymore. Somehow, it made everything worthwhile and, as we stumbled home in the dark, we saw our mud episode in proper perspective.

*   *   *

Some of our autumnal walks simply took us through the village. It was on these walks that we would meet with momentary frustration in the form of the brand new mobile home propped up on pilings, waiting to be hooked up to the utilities. This was the "permanent housing" solution that had finally come in on one of the last summer barges.

Somehow, getting someone with the necessary skills to hook it up defied possibility. No one in the village had ever seen a portable house like this, much less worked on one. There was a mystery about it hard to push aside. So there it sat, minus all the umbilical cords that would link it to mothers Water and Electricity, and that would breathe new life into our confined existence.

Two and a half months turned into three and we knew that pretty soon the ground would be too frozen to permit any of the necessary digging to set it up.

We became jubilant one day after school however, to find a dead ringer for Santa Claus named Al, rummaging around the trailer as if he knew what he was doing. He had flown in from Dillingham and he was going to hook us up.

It might seem pathetic to be so overjoyed by such a mundane event, but we were really looking forward to taking a real shower or bath, using an oven that could accommodate a regular sized loaf of bread, and sleeping in a real double bed. Using adult sized facilities would be a delightful bonus as well.

The additional wait was excruciating, but within another week, we made our big move. It would be a long time before we would take the amenities of civilized living for granted again.

Home Sweet Home!

கூ CHAPTER 8 ல்

"IRPAK" (BIG EYES) IN THE CLASSROOM

It would also be long time before we'd do many things in the normal fashion again. First of all, although teaching is teaching wherever you are, there were definitely some peripheral items that had their own flavor.

To begin with, this was the first time that we couldn't understand our students when they talked among themselves. These children, ranging from ten to fourteen in my fourth-fifth grade combination provided an intense challenge in every way.

While they had entered kindergarten knowing very little English, and while they were now fluent in it, a few refreshing expressions would creep into their animated conversations such as "I'm kidding your leg." Convoluted syntax such as " Where you're going?" and "What we're gonna do?" would insert itself when they asked questions.

Among themselves they still conversed in their mother tongue, Yupik.

At first it was rather unnerving to hear two or three little voices deeply involved in conversation complete with giggles, a collective silent stare, and your name popping up just before more giggles. I was always dying to know what they were saying and I'd give them a mock angry look.

I began to recognize the words for "big eyes" whenever I did that, and was always greeted with peels of laughter at the same time. After a while I managed to learn a few phrases and with the help of my knowledge of French whose sounds are similar to Eskimo, I was able to approximate a convincing set of phrases. In time, the kids began to wonder just how much I did know, and reserved their gossip for places out of earshot.

Another very local aspect of teaching was snack time served at the semi-cafeteria around mid-morning. Like most people, my idea of snack time was milk and cookies (this was before the health food era). I soon learned to savor the all time bush staple: pilot bread. This item could loosely be described as a large, round cracker of a rather substantial toughness that was reputed never to go stale no matter how long it sat on a shelf, in no matter what conditions. It could support mountains of peanut butter, topped with dried raisins or slices of cheese and pseudo-ham. It could be dipped in anything and retain its shape. In fact, I wouldn't have been surprised if it served as a sort of versatile building material.

With the pilot bread, the kitchen servers would whip up powdered milk mixed with a little vanilla to make it more palatable, and serve everybody in little paper cups. The kids would save their cups for the entire school session and make great ceremony of going to the faucet for repeated drinks of water. They seemed to enjoy exclusive ownership of the seemingly most insignificant items, and guarded their little cups jealously. We came to the conclusion that it had something to do with the large size of their families and cultural influence that dictated that they share everything.

The pilot bread snacks lost their surprise value to us after a few days, but we did at least raise our eyebrows when we were served spinach soufflé at ten o'clock in the morning.

Because there happened to be a glut of canned spinach in the storage room, we were to see this unique snack more often than seemed reasonable. If anyone had the childhood horror of it, no one expressed it. We noticed that the inventory in the storage room dictated the trend for snacks for the next week. We were eternally grateful that whoever had made the original order had had no predilection for Brussels sprouts or rutabaga.

*   *   *

"Will we watch a movie?"
"What we're going to watch?"

This was almost a daily question from children whose view of the "outside" was formed exclusively by what they absorbed from the films available from Anchorage through the education department. At first I was shocked when some of the veteran bush teachers mentioned that they used films twice or more times a week. It seemed to us, in our ignorance, like an excuse for not doing a good job teaching.

At the beginning of the school year we put in a substantial film order for the school as a whole. I realized after showing them (very conservatively at first) that they provided a fantastic springboard for all sorts of opportunities. I realized that these films were the only windows to the world at large for these children who were so insulated from it. They could show in fifty minutes what I couldn't do in months, and to this day, I have never seen a finer and more complete collection of educational films than what the "Pictures Inc." service sent us faithfully throughout the entire year. In particular I remember one film called "This is My Country" (the title song) that showed a day in the life of Americans all over the United States (except Alaska). It was so perfect to broaden the scope of these kids who had never been outside their minuscule village. I showed it several times.

In addition to the regular teaching day, several nights a week we held adult education classes. I enjoyed these classes as much or more than the regular ones. The adults would try so hard to do well: to learn English and to do simple computation. The most ingratiating part was how much they showed their obvious enjoyment in coming to school. It was a social event for them and it gave us a perfect chance to get to know one another. Halfway through the evening we would stop classes to have a coffee break and they would always break out in pleased smiles when I asked them in their own language whether they'd like a cup of coffee. I guess my accent was very good because they'd immediately try to begin a conversation in Yupik and, of course, I understood not a word.

࿅ CHAPTER 9 ࿅

NIGHTLIFE IN THE SLOW LANE

A world without T.V.! No way!

It might be difficult for some people to conceive of such a situation. In fact, I know some people who panic at having to be without it for even one evening, let alone months and months.

We never missed it.

The last time we had even cared about watching it was at the time of the first moonwalk, back in July. Fairbanks was one of the few places in the world that did not have live coverage of the event because it had to depend on tapes of world events sent from Anchorage. People in Borneo and Zimbabwe probably saw the event before we were able to. At any rate, the television had not rated high on our entertainment list even when we had access to it, and, now that we didn't, we certainly weren't upset by it. Actually we liked the feeling that the world had indeed "gone away" and felt all the more peaceful for it.

After a few weeks of school, we learned that once a week one of the villagers would show films in his house. These were old movies that had always been the mainstays of the Late and Late Late shows on regular television. The projectionist ordered these films from Anchorage in the same way that we ordered educational films.

Everyone would show up at his front door with a dollar and a mound of candy. After handing over the money at the door, they would crowd into his one-room house and sit on benches that permanently lined his living room. When the benches were full, latecomers would sit anywhere they could. In order not to be overrun with crawling children, we tried to get there in time to get a bench.

It was much more entertaining than the film for us to be part of the weekly ritual that could only take place if the weather allowed the mail plane to bring in the reels.

By being there, we had the opportunity to connect with the entire population of the village. The smaller children would sit on the floor directly in front of the screen, their bright little eyes gleaming in anticipation. The fact that their view from that angle must have been very distorted didn't seem to dampen their spirits a bit. Some of the young mothers also sat on the floor, surrounded by the kids, and usually had one or two on their laps, including a nursing baby. No one seemed to notice the excessive warmth and closeness of the atmosphere that all the bodies were generating in such a confined space.

We noticed throughout the year that westerns were the most appreciated genre and made up the lion's share of the shows. Actually, any kind of good guy-bad guy story was highly acceptable as long as it had good "chase" scenes in it. At the tense moments, you could not hear the dialogue as the entire room would be filled with everyone shouting, " Gikee! Gikee!" ("Hurry! Hurry!") as encouragement for the hero to get away from his pursuers. The smaller children would jump up and down spilling candy and pop in every direction.

Apparently, we were the first teachers to ever join in the film viewing village activity, so, at first we were met with puzzled stares as we entered the "theater." Eventually, people came to expect us. Soon, if we ever missed a session, we had to answer for it.

It was fun to see everyone become so involved in the plots, screaming at tense moments, crying at touching ones, and invariably clapping at the conclusion. The film producers would have been gratified at the reaction of this most appreciative of audiences.

So would the producers of various brands of candy and soda pop. We had never seen so much of either consumed by so few people in such little time. The slurping of the children on their sweets was matched only by the slurping of their tiny siblings nursed by their mothers, mesmerized by the screen. Between that, the noisiness of the projector and the screaming of the audience, the burping, belching, and other emissions, we missed half the dialog of the movies. No matter. We had heard the script a dozen times before, back in so-called civilization. It was the atmosphere that counted anyway.

No matter how old the movie, or how bad, or however stuffy the "theater" had been, we never regretted our evening out on the town and we looked forward to the next time.

* * *

One day, during class, I came to realize how much influence these films had on the population. The kids were quietly doing their work. There wasn't a sound except for an occasional sniff or cough. Without any warning, Thor, the son of the projectionist, who happened to be a developmentally slow child with a developmentally quick sense of humor, suddenly darted out of his chair, backed up slowly in a semi-crouch towards the door leading to the hallway. Brandishing an imaginary six-gun at the class, he slowly pointed it from one side of the room to the other in a wide, all-encompassing semi-circle. In total silence, everyone stared appreciatively as he reached the door, spun his "weapon" and re-holstered it, all in one smooth motion. Without a word, he then turned on his heel and was on his way to the restroom.

Used to his antics, his peers went back to their reading. My mouth stayed open for a few extra seconds until I thought about closing it.

John Wayne certainly would have been proud.

⁊ CHAPTER 10 ⁊

THE STORY KNIFE

No T.V. meant that the children had to be actively involved in their own entertainment. As the movies were only shown once a week, weather permitting—and it didn't always permit, the kids developed creative approaches to dealing with free time. It's one of the sad aspects of today's electronic world that children rarely get a chance to use self-generated imagination.

When we first arrived in Togiak and lived in our classroom "apartment," we would hear the children playing outside the window. Without actually seeing them, it amused me to listen to them speaking their mother tongue because the intonation and sounds reminded me so much of French. In particular, I could hear that one little voice, almost always a girl's, would sound, uninterrupted, for several minutes. This seemed odd because I was used to kids shouting and interrupting each other as a matter of course. After the first voice stopped, another one would begin, and the same thing would happen again.

At one point, not being able to contain my curiosity any longer, I stood up and went to the window to see the sources of the voices.

From my vantage point, looking down over the windowsill, I could see four or five little bodies, crouched low with knees bent, feet flat on the ground, heads tilted in concentration over a spot of mud in the center of the group. One girl was holding something in her hand that she used to make marks in the dirt. At the same time, her voice droned on and on as she held her friends in rapt attention.

Eventually I discovered that they had been taking turns telling stories with the help of their "story-knife," a thin, flat piece of ivory that they used to draw in the dirt to illustrate what they were saying. Sometimes the story-knife was a flat piece of wood or a dull for-real-knife that someone had abandoned. But it was never just a stick. It had to be flat and it had to have a certain feel in order to "tell stories good."

This storytelling actually had much more going for it than its face value of just killing time. In addition to giving the girls a chance to exercise their imaginations, it forced them to practice several skills. As storytellers, not only did they use their creativity of thinking of the plots, and drawing their pictures, (quite often very complicated floor plans of houses), but they honed their speaking skills and acquired a certain stage presence. As listeners, they learned to listen effectively and respectfully, to memorize, to think productively, and to use their own version of "Robert's Rules" during their little sessions. Added to these aspects was the all-important fact that they were preserving and passing on knowledge that they had gleaned from older people, thus keeping the culture alive.

Another skill used in story telling came in the form of a simple piece of string. Almost every kid had a piece of it tucked away in a pocket. It was usually about two feet long, tied in a loop. Most people are undoubtedly familiar with the "cat's cradle," a string game that involves partners transferring the string to each other in a certain pattern. The children here however, were able to make all sorts of patterns by themselves, by manipulating all their fingers in complicated sequence. Each finished pattern represented an item, such as a fish net, a sea bird, a mountain range, and even a rabbit that would "escape" a trap as you pulled on one of the loops.

After learning some of these patterns, I was never without my own piece of string, and, to this day, I can't see a piece of yarn or twine without automatically picking it up and making a "fish net."

String was also an important part of another game called the "Eskimo Yo-Yo." Unlike the conventional yo-yo that involves up and down motion of a single item along the length of a string, the Eskimo version required two items, one at each end of a doubled-up piece of heavy twine, usually the type used for making fishnets. The yo-yos would be very small stuffed animals or objects made of seal or walrus hide, or they would be made into shapes woven from the local grasses. One was attached to one end of about a yard of the twine, and the other was attached to the opposite end. The twine was passed through a little tunnel made of hide that folded the twine into unequal halves. This was the "handle." You were supposed to grasp the handle, and spin the yo-yo in a circle, while holding the other yo-yo still with your other hand. Then you would throw the second yo-yo in the opposite direction and get it spinning too. The trick was to keep them both going in opposite circles by pumping the handle up and down in very vigorous motion. From the front, the viewer sees an optical illusion that the yo-yos bounce off each other, when, in reality, they don't even touch each other.

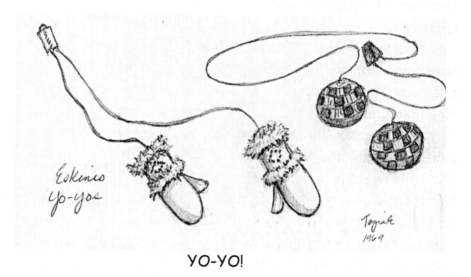

Eskimo
Yo-yos

Togiak
1969

YO-YO!

65

Perhaps the most important activities undertaken by the children and the adults were the local crafts.

Growing throughout the village was an abundance of tall, wide-bladed grass. The women collected bunches of it, dried it until it turned a wheat color and then began a painstaking weaving and coiling system to make all kinds of containers, mostly baskets. In order to add color, they would either dye some of the grass by dipping into water in that they had boiled clothes whose colors ran, or they would dye seal or walrus intestines, cut them into skinny strips to wind around the coiled grass in different patterns. The result was a very decorative watertight container.

Having established a small market for these baskets among the teachers and the visitors to the village, there were always several samples of this "grassware" floating around. Most of the children did not have the patience to make large baskets, so they would use their creativity to make miniature items. They made everything from tiny teapots and cups, to baby rattles, pincushions, and, of course, yo-yos. Hot pads were a popular item because, being flat, they were much easier to make.

Eskimo Grass Basket with seal-gut color bands.

During our year in Togiak, we made several purchases, but the accuracy of hindsight tells us that we didn't come close to buying enough of this craft. There is now an international market for it and the baskets have appreciated a thousand percent.

❧ CHAPTER 11 ❧

GOING WITH THE FLOE

Then there was the time Bob was asked by one of the villagers if he'd like to go on a seal hunt. Bob has never been one to turn down an opportunity to enjoy one of man's macho privileges, so it took him at least a tenth of a second to consider. The only fly in the seal oil was that I wasn't about to let a cultural activity such as this pass me by either. Macho or not, how many people get to hunt seals from a little boat in the frigid waters of the very North Pacific?

In the cultures of the far North, women and seal hunts don't mix. My asking to go along would probably cause a major dilemma for our host. When Bob asked him if I could accompany the men, there was a great deal of chin scratching. After a few exchanges and deliberation, it was determined that I could go. I guess he decided to chalk it up as one more of the white man's eccentricities; women were supposed to handle the catch after it had been taken, never before. If the white man couldn't put his woman in the proper place, then that was his problem. So, it was decided: the woman could go along.

It was impossible to tell when dawn arrived because there was nothing to distinguish the early morning hours from the night. The clouds had an iron grip on the bay. By the time we were ready to go on our first seal hunt, there was a slim gold line separating the earth's horizon and low, heavy overcast sky.

We caught sight of our host, driver and hunting guide all-in-one, Moses, who was busy pushing the skiff toward the water. The beach was now encrusted with a thick, glistening mantle of ice, raggedly extending over the blackness of the water.

Moses' weather-beaten face was what I assessed to be the epitome of the classic Eskimo. Deep and bright dark brown eyes surveyed the horizon as he squinted across the bay. Wrinkles around the eyes contrasted with the taut skin covering the prominent cheekbones and a short, sharp nose. Below, the creases reappeared around a mouth not overly endowed with teeth. In fact, all I could see was one of these in the very front, but I assumed there must have been a few in the back as well. The hands and face were a rich burnished brown, legacy of long hours of exposure to the elements. Straight black hair and a broad grin rounded out the picture.

November had increased winter's hold on our environment and the bay was a silent ballet of floating chunks of blue and silver ice. As we piled into the small riverboat, the distant sun tried valiantly to dissipate the mist, but managed only to bathe the scenery in an eerie silver glow intensified by the reflection of the sea and ice. The noise we made clambering into the boat seemed magnified because of the incredibly deep silence surrounding us.

The silence was torn apart by the roar of the outboard motor. Moses steered us between the small icebergs until we reached open water.

As we looked back at our village for the first time, from this vantage point we were awed by the picture it presented. We had never seen such a variety of hues of blue, silver and gray. The beauty and serenity made our trip worthwhile already, and made us feel an inexplicable kinship with our surroundings.

We sat back, prepared for a relatively long wait for our prey to appear. We were surprised when only a few minutes has passed by an our guide yelled:

"There's one. Quick! Quick!"

The engine stopped. Moses pointed to something in the distance. At about two hundred yards we could see a large ice floe. On the ice floe we could barely make out a small spot of darkness. The boat was still propelled by inertia from the engine, and bobbing up and down because of the action of small waves.

"Get your gun! Get your gun! We go nearer."

With that, Moses fired up the engine and almost ejected us before we had a chance to hang on. He took us up to within a hundred yards and slowed the engine to an idle.

"Shoot! Shoot!"

Moses could hardly contain his excitement. The boat continued to bob up and down while Bob tried to aim his .243 at the now bigger dark spot that was beginning to move. Just as he squeezed the trigger, the boat took a particularly abrupt jump.

We'll never know exactly where the bullet landed. We do know that the seal escaped it as he slithered into the glassy water, never to be seen again.

Moses grinned broadly, flashing his lonely front tooth. "No meat for dinner! We maybe starve tonight!"

He couldn't stop laughing as he revved up the engine. Subtlety was definitely not his forte.

With considerable difficulty, Bob swallowed his pride and we looked around for more ice floes with dark shapes on them. It took a while of circling around at low throttle, but we finally spotted another seal at about a hundred and fifty yards. Again Bob took aim and again the boat foiled his aim. We were beginning to think this might take a little longer than anticipated.

More circling, more squinting, and more bobbing up and down finally brought us within shooting distance of yet another seal who was understandably not threatened by our approach. Wanting my turn to fire a shot, I grabbed the other rifle to try my luck.

By this time, Moses had decided to join in with his own rifle since the pot was still as bare as the old lady's cupboard, and he probably didn't want to lose face at home.

I waited for the boat to be as still as possible, steadied myself, and lined up on the poor animal and fired my first round. There was an immediate spit of ice very close to the seal, who immediately lost his complacency and slid off the floe.

"That was close! That was close! She good shot. Better than you!" More gum, and tooth, and uproarious laughter from our guide.

"Let her try again next time. Maybe we eat tonight!"

Luckily, he missed my normally even-tempered husband's dagger stare. The engine revved again and we were off to scope out a new floe.

By this time the sun had managed to burn off some of the mist and the water reflected the light to such a degree that we had a difficult time looking for our blubbery victims.

It was another long fifteen minutes before we finally spotted another one. This time our guide was taking no chances. Going home empty-handed would have been tantamount to missing a sale on hamburger meat at the local supermarket. We'd had our chance to provide and now it was serious business. Moses nosed the boat as close as he could without alerting the seal.

If you don't get in a lethal shot, the seal will make it to the water and slip away. It either has to be killed instantly so that it never makes it to the water, or it has to be sufficiently wounded that it won't have a chance to exhale in the water and then sink. Its lungs need to remain inflated so that it will float and be easy to retrieve. Our guide whispered: " We all shoot now..."

The rest is history. The hunting gods must have been pleased with us because among the three shots, one found its mark. We were able to scoop up our prey before it submerged. Our guide chuckled happily as he instructed us on how to haul it inside the boat.

How do you grab something that is insulated by an inch or more of fat and covered by slick, wet fur? With centuries of practice, the native people had figured all that out and handled the job with amazing efficiency. There was a tool for every contingency. In this case we used a four-pronged hooking device attached to a small pear-shaped wood float to pull the seal to the boat. We were then instructed to slip a specially fashioned noose around the head and simply pulled the whole thing aboard.

Simple, and no supermarket checkout lines to contend with.

With a mixture of satisfaction and sadness, I contemplated the beautiful animal lying on the bottom of the boat. I hated the idea of killing it, yet I accepted it as the order of life. To those who would find this practice cruel, I would say that the next time they pick out a roast at their local market, they should realize that the slaughter houses that provide the contents of their neatly cellophane-wrapped package operate at a lower level. This animal, that had lived freely to the last instant of its life, would never face a stockyard, nor a slaughterhouse. I looked at it as it lay at my feet and knew that it would contribute in a variety of ways to a system that would make the word "waste" an unnecessary vocabulary item.

Wearily, I leaned back against the stern, enjoying the smooth ride home, grateful that the labor was over.

Actually, it was the easy part that was over. The real labor starts when you get home, and that's when the women come in. It's up to them to make maximum use of the catch. Before anything is done, a few drops of water are sprinkled into the dead seal's mouth in keeping with the old belief that he must not be thirsty on his spiritual trip back to the ocean. After everything is done, his bones will be returned to the sea in order to ensure the continuation of the species. In between, the first step in harvesting the animal is the skinning.

Using her "ulu", a knife made specifically for this purpose, the woman slits the belly skin, careful not to make any more cuts than necessary so as to make maximum use of the entire skin. When she is finished, the skin is stretched over a special frame and looks roughly circular with only three holes in it: one where the face was and two where the front flippers were.

The blubber is cut into strips and put into jars that will be placed behind the stoves to render. The meat is cut into chunks and distributed among relatives. Some is cut into strips for drying. The organ meat is eaten immediately. Because of our standing as members of the hunting party, we were awarded the liver. This was a mixed blessing. Liver is probably the item highest on Bob's hated-foods list.

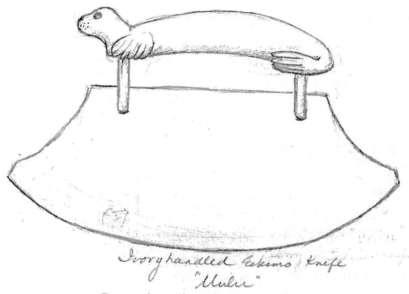

Ivory handled Eskimo "ulu."

We were advised to soak the liver in milk before cooking. This would make it "really good." I must admit that it wasn't without skepticism that I went through the motions of preparing the meal. I knew we could never eat the whole thing, even if it tasted like filet mignon. It must have weighed five or six pounds. We offered part of it to the other teaching couple that accepted it with something short of eagerness. Way short.

After several hours of milk soaking, I sliced the section of meat into what I figured were conservative portions. Luckily, we had just received a box of "fresh stuff" from the itinerant nurse who had stayed with us for her periodic visit to the village. In the box were some beautiful, strong looking onions. I chopped and sliced quite a few of those and fried them along with the meat. Dinner was ready at last.

It's funny how a person who evinces bravery in the face of many dangers will become a pathetic example of abject timidity when it comes to putting something strange in his mouth.

From plate to fork, and fork to Bob's mouth, the first piece of liver made its dubious trajectory. A few tentative chews, and then, wonders of wonders, a beatific smile.

It wasn't bad at all.

In fact it was the mildest and most tender piece of liver we had ever had. Bob was able to eat an entire portion, but he admitted that he would not make it a habit to eat the stuff. True, it was the least objectionable liver he had ever set his teeth into, but he didn't regret his anti-liver diatribe of a few weeks ago when the other teachers and we were discussing the merits of certain foods. He had made his feelings quite clear. Imagine his disconcerted state when, upon accepting a dinner invitation from our fellow-teachers a week later, he faced yet another steaming, onioned-andbaconed dish of seal liver.

I guess either they hadn't been listening, or it was their idea of a joke...

* * *

While we're on the subject of food so close to the heart when meals are often the only highlight of the day, Bob won't forget the time that we were visiting some villagers who happened to be preparing supper. He was asked if he would like some soup. Never wanting to appear contrary, he accepted and was waved over to a large pot boiling on the stove. Grabbing a bowl, he lifted the lid.

"Geez..." he began, a little too loudly to be polite, his eager-for-food look replaced by horror.

He found himself staring at a large eagle claw, emerging talons first, out of the depths of the swirling steam. As the mixture rolled, a beak made a brief but notable appearance as well.

With admirable restraint, and fervently hoping that there was no eyeball floating around, he spooned out a few ladles-worth of liquid and quickly replaced the lid.

Although not really applicable here, we couldn't help thinking that it gave the phrase "eating crow" a whole new meaning. That was the first time that my usually ready-to-eat-anything-husband couldn't even get a spoonful of broth down.

Our courses in culture shock, although quite comprehensive in the "fish" category, had somehow failed to educate us in the "soup" category.

It would be a long time before Bob could lift a lid over a cooking pot with simple pangs of hunger instead of fear.

🙢 CHAPTER 12 🙠

SLEIGH BELLS BUT NO SNOW

It would seem to be a contradiction in terms to have snowless winter vacation in Alaska. Nevertheless, by the third week of December, we wondered with uncertain irony if we'd have a "white Christmas" that year. The weather had been cold, rainy, and extremely windy, but the few snowstorms we'd had never seemed to produce a lasting blanket of the white stuff.

There are at least two or three dozen words for "snow" in the Eskimo language and we were beginning to wonder if some of them were just for wishful thinking.

We had bought ourselves the newest thing for snow transport: a snowmobile, or "snow-go" as the Alaskan term goes.

We hadn't had much of a chance to practice the art of snowmobile riding, and were hoping that we could get in some good mileage on our projected trip to "Twin

Hills," a small one-teacher village that sat across the bay, obscured by a few rolling hills of bare tundra. We had met the teacher on his few trips to our village to obtain school supplies, and we had planned a trip to his place for Christmas Day. Having been confined to less than a square mile area for several months, a short excursion such as this had taken on the dimensions of a major expedition.

We carefully planned our supplies (Christmas dinner), our clothing (snow-pants and Eddie Bauer parkas complete with wolverine and wolf fur ruffs), and transportation (the snowmobile belonging to the two single teachers, plus a sled for two passengers).

By Christmas Eve, we were afraid that our voyage would have to be cancelled because the ground was still only dotted by patches of old crusty snow—the kind that's been thawed and refrozen—sort of like the stuff in your freezer before you clean it out.

Santa Claus had flown in by helicopter the day before from Dillingham, and the entire population of the village had literally slid to the little village store from where he operated out of an old pick up truck. The ground was frozen solid under an inch of "glaciation." If you spread out your coat so that it acted as a sail, and if you were able to keep your balance, you could literally slide for many yards with the wind propelling you: a kind of a land-wind-surfing.

The older villagers depended on "ice grippers" strapped to the soles of their boots to get around. Only the young and miscreants like us kept falling down.

Santa Claus handed out his goodies and flew back to Dillingham. As dusk gathered, we stared a little wistfully at the receding dot that was his helicopter, a little jealous that he would be celebrating the holiday with bright lights and cheer.

We lit our Christmas "bush."

Bob had gone out on the tundra a few days earlier in search of a tree for our living room. He found it to be truly an impossible quest. Nothing on the tundra likes to grow higher than two feet.

After a fruitless search, his snowmobile ski hooked something half buried in the snow and grasses. He pulled at it and, to his delight, realized that a tree had found him. It had originally been some kind of willow with real branches and still bore the vestiges of a few dried up, curly leaves. It had probably come from the riverbed and had been blown or dragged by something. In any case, it was the closest thing to a Christmas tree within five hundred miles, so Bob held on to it tightly all the way home, driving one-handed. I don't think he would have been prouder if he had just managed to spirit away the tree from Times Square. It didn't even look too bad when we decorated it; sort of like the tree Charley Brown had brought home once. Anyway, it did look like Christmas inside the house, if not outside.

Christmas Day dawned bright and breezy but still no precipitation of any kind. Too cold for snow they said.

Undaunted, the four Tundra Troopers prepared the snowmobile caravan for the cross-country trek to Twin Hills School. Bob drove the machine, I sat behind

81

him and the two other teachers rode in the supply sled. At least Bob and I had the benefit of some shock absorbers, but the other two were riding on a piece of plywood fastened to the steel runners trying to span bump after bump of the frozen terrain.

Bob looked (in vain mostly) for the easiest path to follow. Ideally it would have been a path three or four feet wide of compact snow. In actuality there were only occasional patches of crusty, dehydrated snow crystals to try aiming for. The trip was almost as hard on the machine as it was on the posteriors of our passengers. I don't recall the length of time we spent snow-patch-hopping, but we did reach the village in time to reheat the food we had packed and enjoy the parts of the meal that the Twin Hills teacher had prepared. We listened to records, played card games and told stories of our lives "outside." We didn't have a care in our little world, and we thoroughly enjoyed the atmosphere and the company.

After a hot cup of cocoa to gird ourselves for the trip home, we said our good-byes and headed out. By this time the clouds had moved in and, as if ordained by a very poor script, the snowflakes began to fall, gently at first, and then with a vengeance. At the halfway point, the skinny little beam of light projected by our lonely headlight couldn't have picked out the Titanic, let alone the little patches of snow we had found on our way over. The weather had actually warmed up to the point that the snow was not sticking. In other words, instead of providing us with a cushion to make our trip easier, it was blinding us to the extent that we were unable to get our bearings.

Would we be able to celebrate New Year's? Would Bob ever see the present I had ordered for him?

As I hung on to his parka and peered into what I can only call "white darkness," I began to envision the worst of scenarios. I realized then that I had left my mittens behind. I had been hanging on to Bob by putting my hands in his side pockets and I hadn't noticed the absence. I could only imagine what he must be thinking so I never mentioned the mittens. Little things like that in the Arctic have cost more than one or two lives. Tales about such lost lives usually included the word "stupid" repeated several times.

A few more anxious moments of silence passed and I sensed more than heard his exclamation. I opened my eyes as wide as possible and was able to make out a pinpoint of light coming toward us.

Jubilation.

In a moment, we were greeted by two villagers on snowmobiles. They had known we were due back, had seen the blizzard, and had come looking for us. Bob acted as though he had known all along what he was doing. Nevertheless, I have a feeling that he was as greatly relieved as the rest of us were.

Maybe even more.

We thanked the kind souls who rescued us, followed them the rest of the way home, and had some more cocoa before opening our presents in the comfort of our warm, dry living room, by the lights of our decorated Christmas "bush."

It could truly be said that we had not a worry in the world, that we were blissfully happy, and that we were satisfied with the simplest things in life. This was the way we spent our first Christmas in the forty-ninth state, thoroughly believing in the bestowal of good will toward men.

The Tundra Troopers Head Out!
Christmas 1969

⌁ CHAPTER 13 ⌁

HOME BREWING AND BAKING

People often ask us how we could possibly find anything to do "up there" all year long. I don't remember ever being bored even though I can't produce a list of extraordinary activities with which we might have killed time. We enjoyed our privacy, listened to our records, wrote letters, went on walks and altogether enjoyed each other's company. I do know that certain elements of living that take little time normally, took much longer for us.

Daily bread was one of those things. Someone had given me a recipe for bread that required neither milk nor eggs. It usually took me an entire afternoon to bake our bread for the week especially since the first loaf used to disappear almost as soon as it came out of the oven. From that time on, we've been spoiled for the taste of fresh bread. I continued to bake it even after our return to the supermarket world and its packaged goods. Buying it at the store, you miss out on the delight of smelling baking bread that is as much a part of the enjoyment as eating it.

Agreeing that bread is universally basic to life, Bob considers beer a close second. Our village, however, far from providing a store for such things, had an ordinance in effect that banned any alcohol. Thus it was called a "dry village." Part of this stemmed from the influence of the Moravian missionaries who had disseminated their propaganda for decades. (Judging by the amount of blue-eyed people in the villages along the rivers that had served as fairways for the missionaries, propaganda was not the only thing they had spread.)

This religion not only banned all elements of the ancient cultures such as the songs and the dancing, but allowed nothing to replace them either. They had effectively wiped out any type of activity people inherently enjoy to show happiness and to keep the culture alive. When the kids used to come to our trailer for their Sunday "wisits," they would ask us to play our records.

Timidly at first, almost furtively, they would tap their feet to the music and gradually work up to dancing all over the living room with exuberance and abandon. They knew it was against the church rules, and the forbidden aspect probably made it all the more delicious to them. They never tired of listening to the same records over and over again.

We hated to kick them out after a couple of hours of this, but we became tired of hearing the same music, and we had to limit the Sunday visits or our visitors would have stayed well into the evening.

Judging by the events "wet villages," we had to admit that the banning of alcohol was a beneficial institutional legacy, but Bob didn't appreciate the regulation as it applied to him. Never daunted by the constraints of society, he decided to apply one of the

Can we come in and wisit?

Alaskan principles we were beginning to appreciate: if you can't buy it, get it, or steal it—make it.

Our trailer had a guest bedroom and bathroom at one end. We used the bedroom to store our canned goods. The bathroom became our brewery that was presently filled with bottles of every type that we had been saving for a while in anticipation of this experiment.

Bob had obtained a recipe for dark beer, and used the precious yeast that had been originally designated for our bread supply. He had bought hops and malt before we had left Anchorage, as well as an all-important hydrometer. We had two big plastic garbage cans in which he mixed the brew until that perfect moment arrived as determined by the reading on the hydrometer. At this time it was to be poured into bottles and capped with our handy bottle-capper, also purchased on our original supply trip.

We waited for the appropriate aging process. Bob would go into the bathroom every day and stare longingly at the bottles. I don't know what he was expecting to see, but whatever it was, he didn't see it because he'd always return empty handed and droopy-mouthed.

He shouldn't have bothered because we were spared any more guessing when, one night, as we were dozing off, we were jarred to the waking world by a loud popping sound, similar to a pistol shot. We sat up wondering what crazy person was shooting a gun.

Suddenly it sounded as though an army was having target practice. Really alarmed by now, we ran to the living room to look out the large windows.

It was then than we realized that the war was taking place in the back bathroom. Unlike the wine of TV commercial fame, the beer was obviously not going to wait until its time. We rounded the doorway with caution in time to be greeted by projectile bottle caps bouncing off the walls and ceiling. Geysers of amber liquid and froth exploded like the biggest New Year's celebration ever held. As we looked at this labor of love disintegrating before our eyes, and envisioning the cleanup job that lay ahead of us, Bob could only lamely admit that he guessed he had used too much yeast. Next time he'd have to be more scientific about it.

It was weeks before we could get rid of the smell.

Years later, we heard that the kids who used to come and "wisit" us on Sunday afternoons, who had long been told of the inherent evils in alcohol, told the teachers who replaced us," They made BEER back there..." while pointing a shaky finger at the dark hallway, their eyes big and round in a sort of reverent awe.

* * *

The next night, I was awakened again. This time by my husband letting out a very odd bellow and jumping around on our bed in a very good imitation of a Mexican jumping bean.

"Get him! Get him!' he was yelling as he stepped all over me and dove to the floor. Bush living had gotten the better of him. He had finally snapped.

"Calm down. What's going on? Are you having a nightmare or what?"

I was really getting worried at his behavior. He was crawling around on the floor, head down, posterior in the air, whacking away at something with one of his boots.

"Get that empty coffee can! Quick! He's gonna get away!

"What's gonna get away?" I yelled fearfully, remembering a bout of sleepwalking he had once suffered from.

"I don't know! Whatever was just sitting on my chest blinking his beady eyes at me! Hurry up! I've got him cornered."

Well, might as well humor him.

I stumbled to the kitchen to find the can and handed it to him a little fearfully. He turned it upside down with a vengeance.

"Get in there, you little piece of vermin!"

By the time things had calmed down and we'd slipped something over the opening to make sure the victim couldn't escape, Bob's breathing had returned to normal.

"God, that scared me. Something woke me up, and I looked down at my chest and there's these shiny little eyes looking at me. And his nose is going like mad."

We carefully looked inside the can.

At the bottom sat a small furry creature, not the least bit frightening looking, blinking his eyes and wiggling his (or her) nose.

"That little thing frightened you?" I could barely suppress a laugh.

"Well, it looked a lot bigger when it was two inches from my face," came the indignant reply. "It could've bitten my nose off."

Later, after looking up arctic rodents, and putting him in one of the classrooms, we found out that it was either an arctic vole or a lemming. I leaned toward the latter, thinking that instead of jumping off a cliff in the mass suicide that these little animals are known to commit in order to combat over-population, this one had almost met his Waterloo of being inhaled in the snort of a sleeping snorer.

What an ugly end it would have been for such a cute little creature.

* * *

You might think that, being tucked away in the epitome of remoteness we'd never get a chance to see many outsiders. Nothing could be further from the truth. In the government's infinite wisdom, it provided us with a steady stream of visitors whose job descriptions covered every aspect of good old American bureaucracy. While the Public Health Service was responsible for the lion's share of visitors, we were also graced by the presence of social workers, tax investigators, Bureau of Land Management surveyors, census takers, building inspectors, ad infinitum. We were so tired of making polite conversation and preparing extra meals that there were a few weeks during the winter that we prayed for inclement weather so that the air taxis couldn't fly in more "guests." That hardly ever occurred. It wasn't that the weather was always great; it was just that the pilots were too skilled.

After a visit by one of the aforementioned service-people, we were afraid that the weather would be too bad for our guest to leave. We shrank at the thought of having to make polite conversation for a longer stretch of time and deplete our food supply further. This sounds grossly inhospitable, but when you have a limited supply to begin with, you become very parsimonious about handing it out. People who are used to this type of itinerant life, such as the doctors and nurses, often bring a huge case of "fresh stuff" as payment out of their per diem. Others, however, liked to pocket their per diem and live off our generosity. At first we just accepted this, but as our supplies dwindled and we were reduced to canned artichoke hearts for vegetables, we began to present bills to those who weren't aware of "bush etiquette."

At any rate, while the weather was never bad enough to keep people away, it worked both ways: it was almost never bad enough to prolong their visit either. In this instance, the winds were gusting to seventy knots across the main runway. There was a very seldom-used small cross strip by the west-end of the village that would have to be used in today's crosswind.

His stomach filled with our groceries, our guest took his leave, blessed either by nerves of steel or by incredible naïveté.

We watched out our bedroom window as he was blown over to the airplane. We had seen some touchy takeoffs but felt that this was probably the most marginal flying weather yet. We felt sorry for our ex-guest as the engines revved and the plane taxied to the tip of the cliff at one end of the cross strip. Below was the ice-covered bay. The engine, muted by the wind whipping the sound away, strained against it. The plane inched its way forward, barely clearing a few yards when it lifted and we held our breath as it actually flew backwards. We wondered at this phenomenal display of aerodynamics. The plane gained altitude, banked to one side, and fought its way towards Dillingham.

I was wondering if our groceries were still in the passenger's stomach.

꙾ CHAPTER 14 ꙮ

MEDICINE MAN IN SPITE OF HIMSELF

In many small villages, a teacher's job involved a great deal more than the business of the classroom. Often the general population was illiterate, and the teacher was asked to interpret all paperwork. If there was a question about village government, his or her advice was sought. As the sole formally educated person, the teacher was often regarded as the final authority where many things were concerned.

This was a mixed blessing. In some villages, especially those with only a teaching couple, some teachers were known to abuse their so-called authority by trying to become "great white fathers." They would insist on having their say in absolutely everything that went on in the village, and impose their decisions on everyone. Reluctant to complain to the school authorities because they felt incompetent in the world outside, the villagers would often accept the situation and hope that the offending person would eventually be transferred. Sometimes this did happen, but often the situation remained the same for years as the teacher enjoyed his power.

In our situation, things were a little different because the village was larger, some of the people had come from elsewhere, and some had received some elementary education. Simultaneously, there was an underlying "native power" movement in evidence throughout the state and it was having a small, but perceptible impact here. A few of the village leaders were quite firm in maintaining their autonomy, and our principal teacher, whose legal authority was limited to the physical plant of the school only, found his "great white father" tendencies thwarted. He tried to impose several things on us also, such as our submission to him of daily lesson plans and a dress code. At first our ignorance allowed us to submit, but after several conversations with other teachers at a few workshops we attended, we discovered that he had no business requiring anything of the kind. In order to keep things smooth, we accepted things we could stand, and simply did what we wanted in other cases.

Whereas at first the many public health officials routinely stayed with the "head teacher" as a matter of tradition, we found that, either they must have found some elements of hospitality lacking, or they were getting tired of the same accommodations, because more and more often they stayed with us for every trip to the village. In fact, we became fast friends with the itinerant dentist, nurse and doctor. Most of them lived permanently in Dillingham, the base from which they traveled to the outlying villages. So we always had plenty of places to stay if we needed them in Dillingham or Anchorage. As a bonus, we learned a great deal about medicine and health care, subjects that had always interested both of us.

Sometimes, through the schools short wave radio, we had to relay emergency procedures in a three-way conversation from a very remote village, to us, to the hospital in Dillingham, and back again. We fervently hoped that nothing was lost in the translation because, as can be observed from the following reenactment, some of the medical problems from the villages were truly amazing.

Crackling voice over the radio from a remote village:

" This person, he have problem with big long...in " ... static..." Over."

Bob: " Say again. Say again. We didn't get the message. Say again."

Remote voice: "Where the doctor is? Need doctor right away for ..." static..." very long and dark..." static... " and feel very much bad. Over."

Bob: "The doctor is NOT here. We have to relay message to the hospital in Dillingham. Tell me the problem so I can tell the doctor. Over."

Indignant remote voice: "Why doctor not there? Need very much. We...static...pull it out but... break ... and he [or she] very much yelling..." static.

Bob (frustration beginning to tell): "What broke? Where is it? What's wrong? You have to tell me so I can tell the doctor. Over."

Remote voice, now very indignant: "... said the doctor NOT there. Now he there? This person... out of her butt and need to ... pull it out. Very weird and very much need doctor. Over."

Bob (slightly blue in the face): "Doctor is in Dillingham. I need to radio him. Did you say somebody has something growing out of her butt? Please say again so I can tell doctor. Over."

Static and voice: "... something weird growing out of butt. Need pull out... too slippery. What we do? Over."

Bob, (now slightly red): "Okay, Okay. I am sending message to doctor. Stay by the radio for next message. Over."

It took a half-hour to relay the information back and forth from the other village, through our radio to Dillingham. By the time it was over, the descriptions relayed over the air should have singed the ear hairs of any officer of the Federal Communications Commission who might be listening. I don't remember if the ailment was ever diagnosed, but we were certain it merited its own chapter in the Journal of the American Medical Association.

* * *

Our medical responsibilities did not end with the radio. One evening, the head teacher knocked on our door. Behind him, smiling politely, stood an older lady from the village. Obviously hating to relinquish his status as highest exalted authority figure, our colleague grudgingly asked if we knew anything about giving injections, because this lady needed her penicillin shot, and he wasn't prepared to do it. He had asked her to wait for the village health aide only to find that she was out of town having a baby.

Bob had had experience working in a hospital many years ago, but really didn't relish the idea of putting a needle in the emaciated arm insistently proffered him by the lady. She was determined to get her medicine no matter what.

So, leading his smiling victim, and trying to look as confident as Florence Nightingale in a parka and snowmobile boots, Bob trudged over to the nurse's office in the school where he tried to inflict the least damage possible with the injection.

He was relieved to have it over with, and had forgotten about the incident until we received a knock on the door the next night. There stood his patient, smile and arm all ready for a repeat performance.

We were well aware that penicillin was dispensed with amazing freedom, but had always thought that one injection would take the place of a ten-day series of pills even here.

But the lady insisted that she needed another one.

Bob looked at the arm that now had a rather large discolored area threatening from shoulder to elbow. He looked so pathetic that someone might have mistaken him for the person at the wrong end of the syringe.

Looking fearfully at the lady with the encouraging smile, he knew getting out of another medical contribution was impossible. So, once more, he made the trek over to the medicine chest, victim in tow.

He was gone ten minutes.

"Don't ask," he warned darkly in answer to my quizzical look as he returned from the school, medical kit in tow.

Later, he explained, "She'll probably be back tomorrow so I decided to save us a trip and just do it here. I think she's addicted to the needle."

I had to admire the lady's bravery.

* * *

The villagers' approach to medicine was a mixture of old ways and new.

One evening, at an adult education class, I noticed that one of the ladies had an ugly cut on her hand that was itself extremely swollen. I could see red lines of infection extending to her elbow where they were obscured by her sleeve. Around her wrist she had tied a single strand of red yarn in a loose knot.

I asked her about the yarn and gathered from her explanation that the yarn was to prevent the infection from going higher—sort of a symbolic barrier to

99

infection. I didn't feel it necessary to draw her attention to the fact that the infection, already manifest well past the yarn, was not paying proper allegiance to the proposed defense. I just insisted pretty firmly that she see the health aide the next day for a good shot of the miracle drug. I knew she was safe from my husband's well intentioned, and, ostensibly adequate ministrations, because the health aide had returned to the village by this time.

I was relieved to see my "student" in the office the next day. Apparently, she had decided that modern medicine might work well in conjunction with the yarn still tied around her wrist.

꧂ CHAPTER 15 ꧁

THE CURE

Give and take is universal and Bob's involvement in the health field was no exception. He found himself slightly congested one evening and it did not escape our old hunting guide Moses' notice. Insisting that he knew how to take care of it, he told Bob to meet him at his house the next night.

"We give you good steam bath in the "maqui" [mah-kee], he counseled. "Tomorrow night, your cold all gone. For sure, for sure."

He slapped Bob on the back and exploded into one of his uproarious laughs.

We got the distinct feeling that the real picture was escaping us.

The steam bath was the villagers' only bathing method, and was usually a family affair.

The structure itself was made of four sheets of plywood lying lengthwise to the ground so that it was only four feet high. The roof was usually another piece of plywood covered with small bits of corrugated tin roofing. The inside was roughly divided into two compartments: one, a kind of a mini-locker room where you took off your clothes and shoes, and the other, the main steaming compartment. The principle in effect here was: the smaller the area to heat, the quicker and more effective the steam bath.

It was quite a trick to get an entire family around the fifty-gallon drum, lying on its side, radiating intense heat in an area no bigger than two or three bathtubs.

In order to intensify the heat, someone would pour water over the length of the stove, instantly bathing everyone in a boiling cloud of steam. Everyone was to sweat away all the impurities, including disease, and rinse off with a little water from a ladle. As wood for fuel in a treeless environment was at a premium, consisting of all the driftwood family members could find on the beach, the steam bath was to be treasured and used to its maximum at each session. Once lit, families might go in shifts or divide into gender groups with other families until the last heat molecule could be coaxed from the fuel supply.

Armed with the knowledge of the significance of being invited to participate in this family ritual, Bob felt honored and looked forward to it with his customary eagerness to experience life's riches. What escaped him was that it was also to be a kind of initiation rite to test the white man's mettle. That he could withstand cold was a forgone conclusion as attested to by his many excursions in the wilderness. But could he withstand the rigors of total cleansing by fire? That was the question soon to be answered by nightfall of the next day.

Donning underwear, a shirt, jeans, and his cowboy boots, the soon-to-be-cured-of-what-ailed-him unsuspecting victim headed for the house where he was to meet his host.

Having met, they both walked over to the steam bath, several hundred yards from the house. Bob hadn't taken his parka because the distance was short and the parka would have proved cumbersome. He was becoming aware of the ever-increasing cold however, and was glad when his host motioned for him to enter the squat structure ahead.

Bending over almost double to get in the doorway, he wrestled out of his clothing before entering the steam room. The fire must have been going for quite a while judging by the suffocating heat.

Not knowing which people were already enjoying their cleansing, he didn't know whether or not to strip completely, and started to go in with his jockey shorts still on. He felt a jerk and turned to find his host gesturing to remove the obviously offending item.

Literally in no position to discuss the matter, he complied and entered the second chamber. At the same time, he made the mistake of inhaling. His lungs immediately registered their indignation and he was afraid they'd go on immediate strike. He fought to get another breath and was amazed to find himself alive.

There was no one in the room so he moved to the side to allow his host to follow. The heat was more intense than anything he had felt before, and he wasn't sure if he would last enough time to effect a cure for his congestion.

After settling down in the small space, he was joined by more villagers, the first in a procession of bathers, all men. Each time another came in, Bob was forced to move farther back into the suffocating recesses of the room. He wondered that there was enough oxygen to go around.

After ten minutes, there were six glistening bodies packed around the fire not unlike the hot dogs of the "they plump when you cook 'em" commercial.

"Now you get better," intoned the host.

He pulled out a bottle of pine sol cleaner, ceremoniously unscrewed the cap, and slowly poured the contents on the top of the red-hot drum.

Bob figured the germs in his passages were supposed to die of shock because that was the only plausible explanation for the curing process. If the loud hiss of noxious steam didn't scare you to death, the acrid atmosphere would take care of it.

Bob tried to hold his breath but finally gave in to his reflexes. He tried one little breath and lived.

Surreptitiously observing his fellow bathers, he found that they seemed engrossed in conversation, unaware of his acute discomfort, and, more amazingly, totally devoid of discomfort of their own. He noted that they were as pale as he was and that it must be their constant exposure to the elements that gave them such dark skin on their hands and faces.

They tended to their bathing.

Breathing in a most gingerly fashion, Bob watched as they scraped their skin with a blunt knife blade, occasionally rinsing with a few precious drops of water.

Mainly you were supposed to sweat yourself clean.

Judging by the copious amounts of sweat he was generating, Bob figured this was the cleanest he'd ever been.

After five more minutes of par boiling, he finally decided that if his germs weren't all dead, they deserved to live forever. He, for one, needed some regular air if he was going to outlive them. Voice slightly hoarse, he announced that he had had enough and indicated that he was leaving, ostensibly to make room for the next group.

Slithering by the other slimy bodies he made it to the outer section where he began searching for his clothes. Had he known that so many people would be using the steam bath, he probably would have made a point to make a neat pile of his clothes. As it was, he had to rummage around to find his boots and slip them on.

Bent over double, he was in the middle of trying to thread one booted leg through the leg hole of his jockey shorts when his host entered the outer "changing room" and admonished him, "You no put on clothes. Go out right now to my house."

With that, Moses scooped up his own neat pile of clothes and took off down the path with only his slippers on, leaving behind a man as perplexed as he was naked.

With one leg still through the leg hole of his undershorts, Bob analyzed the quandary in which he found himself. Did he suffer from ridicule of those who wondered why he was trying to clothe himself in the cramped and traffic-plagued outer steam room, or did he follow his host through the streets of the village risking exposure?

A vision of newspaper headlines flashed before him: "Teacher Dies of Indecent Exposure," or worse, " Teacher From Up North Exposes South Face."

He decided to hotfoot it (poor choice of idiom considering the ice-covered path) to his host's house. He started hesitantly up the path.

Almost immediately he heard the murmur of young voices in deep conversation coming his way. In abject horror he realized the voices belonged to two of his oldest students, two pretty girls of sixteen or so.

He glanced to the right.

Too late to run up the path in competition with the bright full moon. All he could do was to try to reenter the steam bath in utmost haste. By this time however, the body traffic was such that the only part of the body he was able to conceal was his head.

While he was in this way epitomizing ostrich behavior: his head inside the outer room of the steam bath, the rest of him exposed to the outside elements, he lamely muttered something about a lost sock, hoping that his actions would thus be legitimized.

After sufficient time had passed for the girls to be far enough away, he "found" the offending sock, checked his avenue of escape, and clomped his way to the house of his long gone host, grimly determined that no one else would see him in this compromising position.

What were the reactions of his students going to be when he saw them in class the next day? Already he blushed furiously at the thought of the giggling that would go on at his expense.

(As he found out later, the giggling was aimed at his futile and inexplicable attempt to hide, rather than on the natural state of his being naked: "Mister Norberg, how come you go back in maqui even though you finished?" Nothing would have been mentioned if he had casually followed his host and merrily waved a greeting.)

Having arrived on his host's outside porch, he hopped around, trying not to lose his grip on his outer clothing and trying once more to insert his legs in his now rather stiffly frozen underwear.

Through the small window, he had caught sight of his host at the back of the house, still unclothed, drinking something from a cup. He seemed to be in conversation with someone, but before Bob had succeeded in donning the ever-elusive clothing, he heard a yell bidding him to come in for tea.

Still feeling frustratingly under-dressed for the occasion, Bob entered the house only to be greeted by the entire family including grandma, who beamed her smile at him.

After his bitingly exhilarating jog through the frigid night air, the house seemed extremely warm. Bob felt slightly overcome by it all.

Still fiercely clutching the trappings of civilization to his sweaty chest, he gladly accepted the cup of tea offered him.

He suppressed a wince at the first mouthful; there was as much sugar as tea in his cup. He managed to down it and then casually slip on his clothes, all the while carrying on a conversation in unconcerned manner.

He finally took leave of his hosts with the latter's assessment of his fortitude ringing in his ears, "You do pretty good maqui tonight. Pretty good for a white man!"

It was then that he realized he had been on a trial of sorts, and took the praise to heart.

Later on, in the privacy of our bedroom, Bob took off his shirt and we were both amazed, if not a little horrified, at the violent mottling of his skin by all the surface capillaries. We could only guess that the heat had been so intense, that the capillaries closest to the surface of the skin had expanded to bursting.

As for his nasal passages... well... for the first time in many months, that night I wasn't plagued by his customary snoring. I entertained thoughts of forcing him to undergo this treatment at every opportunity so that I could sleep better henceforth. The reception I got after voicing this opinion made me realize that the line between macho-ism and masochism is quite sharply delineated.

ᘓ CHAPTER 16 ᘗ

THE GIFTS OF SPRING

Time began to slip by quickly as it's prone to do when your routine rolls on. By spring, we had to decide whether we'd stay in this village for another year or whether we'd like to try somewhere else.

We loved the life here, it's unhurried pace, and the cocoon of beneficial isolation it provided us in the high blood pressure cauldron of the outside world. We realized just how removed we had been when we didn't know until months later that an important political figure had died.

109

If our association with the other teachers had been a closer one, we might have undertaken another year, but we were beginning to miss having conversations and friendship with others of similar tastes. In addition, as much as we enjoyed teaching these elfin characters of elementary age, we were interested in returning to the age group for which we had been trained, ie. high schoolers.

Through our summer orientation program, we had made friends with several other teachers, some of whom had been stationed at one of the area high schools in the interior of the state. We decided to apply for a transfer to one of these.

While we waited for the paperwork to go through, we made the most of our last few months on the tundra. Sunday "wisits" with our students continued. We usually let about five "wisitors" in at a time and they would stay for an hour or two.

One of these almost touched off a diplomatic incident when, during the course of our conversation, the subject of babies came up. The kids had decided that something wasn't quite right because whenever teaching teams came to the village, they were always childless. Not realizing that the state preferred this in the couples that were sent to remote areas, they felt that this was an oddity that bore correcting. One of the kids asked me why we didn't have any children of our own, and before I could produce a reasonable answer, Bob made some wisecrack halfway under his breath intended for my ears only.

I don't remember his exact words, but before I could stop her, one of the little girls got up and ran down the hall to the door.

"I'll be right back," she yelled. "I'll go ask my Dad to help you. He knows how to have babies good."

This was undoubtedly a reference to her impressive number of siblings.

Luckily, she had problems with the door handle and we were able to intercept her.

I had read the old tales of Eskimo comprehensive hospitality to strangers, and I did not want to cause hard feelings because of my own ethnic hang-ups.

As the days grew longer and the winds died down, we spent more time outdoors enjoying the environment any way we could.

Some of the people who stayed with us periodically for whatever reason, had airplanes of their own. They repaid us for our hospitality by flying us around the countryside. We were able to fly over the Walrus Islands where thousands of these animals had been slaughtered by the natives for nothing but their tusks. Carving ivory, originally an art developed in the northern regions of the state, was beginning to flourish here. The money was good and the resources plentiful, for now. It was sad to see the carcasses rotting on the beaches, especially when we knew that tons of meat were being wasted, and that the substantial part of the tusk in the skull was not even harvested because it was easier simply to saw the visible part at the jaw-line.

We saw seal rookeries, thousands of birds, and a grizzly who stood up on her hind legs and swiped at our low flying 'plane. We visited other small villages including Platinum, named after the mining done in that area for the mineral.

Our appreciation for the scenery was boundless. We were gratified as we flew over acres and acres of unspoiled land that the world contains such a place and that we were connected to it. Much of the land had never been marred by a single human footprint, and probably never will. It was comforting in a way, and deliciously forbidding in another. The only thing separating us from total union with the powerful environment was the single engine that suspended us in fragile safety. This feeling of "on the edge" was a constant companion throughout our years in Alaska. One minute you're a spectator, but in the next, you might be engineering your survival because of malfunctioning machinery. We learned eventually never to take anything for granted. I did say "eventually," so that's another story.

*   *   *

Springtime in the village meant ice fishing. Equipment needed for the successful execution of this sport was a large Blazo can (liquid fuel for lanterns etc.) to sit on, a piece of fishing line, and a bent fork tine tied to the end of it. Lots of warm clothes and good boots stood to make the experience more enjoyable. If you were unlucky, you'd need a fair share of patience, too.

As with everything else in the survival game, there's a scientific approach to the task at hand, that comes only with experience.

Bob and I headed for the happy fishing grounds on the frozen slough behind the village. As we had seen earlier, the slough served as harbor for the riverboats during the summer, but in the winter, it served as a recreation area. Now that the smelt run had started, the glaciated area was dotted with fishing holes. Hardly larger than sardines, smelt make a very good meal if you catch a large number. Otherwise they'll serve only as hors d'oeuvres.

Not knowing the second thing about fishing of this type (we did know the first: find a hole in the ice), we selected two holes within talking range. We turned our large can-seats over so that we could sit on them, unraveled our fishing line, and dropped the makeshift fishhooks down the fishing holes.

I had observed other people giving little jerks to their lines and did the same. In a few moments, I felt a miniature tug on the line. I stood up as I withdrew the line from the hole, disbelieving. It had been such a weak tug that I was sure it had only been the current under the ice.

Glistening in the afternoon sun's rays however, the smelt on my fork tine twisted and turned in the breeze. I unhooked it and put it in a large baggie I had brought.

Bob continued to fish.

I repeated the operation. Less than a half a minute later, another tug, and another fish.

Bob was still intent on his fishing hole.

Again I immersed the fishhook only to pull it back up, loaded again. The freezer bag was filling up. Every minute produced a fish on my line.

Bob continued to concentrate.

I asked to borrow his baggie because mine was full. It wasn't my intent to add insult to injury; I really did need another bag.

He grunted his assent and kept staring at the little opening in the ice.

By the time I had filled both baggies to the bursting point, Bob's hook was still only threatening the deep.

The sun had set and a cold breeze had picked up. I announced that I'd go home and prepare the dinner that was already "in the bag," so to speak.

Another grunt. The hole was still silent.

I headed for home, mentally putting together the ingredients for dinner. The fish were too small to clean the normal way, so I simply cut off the heads and tails and dredged them in flour. I prepared vegetables and waited for Bob to return.

After another hour of waiting, I decided to take him another freezer bag and help him bring home the "seats" and the fish.

Too late.

As I opened the door, I saw, as he stood there, that he didn't need any help. There was nothing except the two "seats" to carry.

114

Ice fishing

Dinner was a somber affair. If we had known the inside information about smelt fishing on the slough, we could have spared a very beleaguered male ego.

Below the surface, the ice is not smooth and straight. Instead, it's riddled with canals that provide little thoroughfares for the fish. Because the would-be fishermen can't see the canals, they make the holes randomly. Holes only a foot apart can produce totally different yields, as had been depressingly illustrated by the ones we had selected. Obviously, my hole had been dug squarely over a good canal. The other one had probably never yielded anything because the ice was thick to greater depth, thus frustrating the fishes' progress in that direction.

The fish didn't have a monopoly on frustration, either. Just ask the guy who sat freezing his appendages off, waiting for them to come by...

* * *

That spring, someone in Dillingham was offering a course through the University on "Higher level thinking for the classroom." Not wanting to miss a chance to further our intellectual growth, we decided to make the trip to the big town for the two weekends necessary to complete the course.

Actually, it provided an excuse to soothe incipient cases of "cabin fever." I'm sure that this aspect serves as part of the rationale for offering these courses to bush teachers. The State and the University knew that a little "R and R" for people who hadn't been out of their villages for six or seven months, might make them more likely to repeat the stint if they could party a little.

At any rate, that was our reasoning and we jumped at the chance. The next "hole" in the weather allowed the mail plane to scoop us up and drop us off in Dillingham for a weekend of welcome change.

The course was valuable on its own, but we found the informal discussions among teachers stationed in the area to be of even greater value. We were able to compare notes, to make and renew friendships, and generally to enjoy a social smorgasbord of old and new acquaintances. Time had come for us to collect on hospitality debts that the steady procession of health care workers etc. had incurred during their stays on our turf for the past school year. The place seemed chock-full of individuals with strong and interesting personalities. Maybe it was the extreme conditions, or the length of time we had gone without any social feedback, but everyone seemed to be so vigorous and almost larger than life.

We ended up corresponding for many years with people we had known only two days. We felt reassured about human nature.

The world couldn't be a bad place as long as people like that existed.

❦ CHAPTER 17 ❧

SWITCHING GEARS

One day, the mailbag contained our transfer approval. We were to teach at an area high school in the village of Tanana. We broke out the map in order to locate it.

The easiest way to find the spot is to point where you think the exact center of the state is. You'll see it right at that point, at the confluence of the Tanana and Yukon rivers, about 120 air miles west of Fairbanks.

That would be a change. We'd miss the ocean, but trees would be a plus.

Another change would be the number of teachers at the school that included all twelve grades plus kindergarten. There were at least a dozen of them, and we knew one of the teaching couples well. Our social life was obviously going to pick up considerably.

In the few weeks that remained we had to make an important decision. We knew we'd be going back "outside" to visit friends and relatives before returning to Fairbanks for added graduate courses in summer school towards the Master's degrees we wanted. We had become extremely found of a little girl in my class named Judy. A very quick mind set her apart from her peers and we developed a special relationship with her because we shared mutual enjoyment in each other's company. She was so willing to learn and wanted so much to see the world outside her village. She would never tire of asking questions until finally we came up with the idea that maybe she should see everything first hand, but we had no idea how taking her with us for a cross-country trip would be viewed by her family. We put the question to her and her eyes glowed.

No problem there.

We asked her to speak to her parents about it. This might prove more difficult.

People in the village had ideas about children that we sometimes found hard to accept. One of the ladies, whose sister-in-law couldn't have children, became obligated to give her the next infant she gave birth to.

She did as was expected and gave up her next baby daughter. From then on, she lived her daily life next door to her own daughter whom she had to call "niece." She had absolutely no say in whatever decisions were made about the child, and had to constantly restrain herself when she could see that the decisions were bad.

Children were often shuffled around for reasons we never understood. By taking another family's child with us, we weren't sure how our intentions might be interpreted.

119

In a kind of three-way indirect diplomacy that lasted a couple of weeks, we were eventually given permission to make it happen. All three of us were elated at the prospect. We couldn't wait to show our little traveler-to-be all the sights of the outside world.

* * *

In the meantime, we had thirteen cans of pineapple, chunk style; seven cans of pineapple, sliced; four cans of Spam; two boxes of potato buds; six boxes of powdered "Milkman;" and other assorted containers of food to get rid of before we left. We held a little food sale in our guest bedroom and everybody came. By the time the last customer had left, we wondered that the furniture was still in its place. There wasn't a can of mandarin orange segments or pieces and stems of mushrooms in sight. Nothing would ever go to waste, we knew, and felt good that some families would have extra special meals with the variety of items they had obtained thanks to our "sale."

We had used our thirty dozen eggs throughout the year except for the last dozen or so that were a little too "strong" even for our accustomed tastes. An old refrigerator in one of the school's storage rooms had housed our case of thirty dozen eggs. To keep them edible all year, we faithfully turned each box over periodically so that the yolks would never rest in the same position for more than a week. This was a little trick we had learned from some experienced people, and hadn't really believed it would work.

After nine months, we were true believers. The slight greenish tinge that appeared about February didn't faze us at all. The eggs looked fine after they had been cooked and we found later on that fresh eggs tasted awfully flat.

We traded what was left of our frozen side of beef to one of the village families for a beautiful grass basket. It's now worth three or four whole cows. It completed our collection of local arts and crafts, the ivory carvings and the many different items woven from the long, windblown tundra grasses that grew like tall spears along the beach.

We were afraid that time would erode the progress of the local art because the younger people seemed reluctant to spend time on continuing the heritage. We made sure that we had representative samples of everything. The sentimental value of the objects was greater to us than what they would fetch on any market.

The second to last week in May saw us climb aboard our last flight from Togiak to Dillingham. This time we had our little companion in tow. We looked down on our little square mile of world, the only world Judy had known for eleven years, and the one we had known barely eleven months. We knew we'd miss the incredible security this private corner of the universe had afforded us. What we didn't know was that the safety, freedom, and complete peace we had enjoyed, we'd never again experience.

In our ignorance, and with a melancholy backward glance through the scratched airplane window, we closed this chapter of our lives in innocent comfort, and left Togiak to the gathering low clouds.

Indian
mukluks
KN

❧ CHAPTER 18 ❦

REVERSE CULTURE SHOCK
(OR "SORRY. IF YOU HAVE NO CREDIT
CARD, YOU DON'T EXIST.")

When you've been out of circulation for a while, culture shock happens in reverse. What had been normal in your life before the change takes getting used to when you're plunged back into it. The crowds, the lines, the traffic, and the fast pace of life all seemed unreal. The supermarket was downrightly intimidating. The regular-size bottles of ketchup were cute and liquid milk tasted odd. We had forgotten what a fresh head of lettuce looked like. On our first grocery excursion, we did more gawking than buying.

Our primary stop after Anchorage was to be Seattle, where we planned to buy a car for our trip across the "lower 48."

We flew into Seattle after dark, around midnight, and as we broke out of the clouds, Judy let out a loud squeal as she saw the wide expanse of city lights spread below us. Since Togiak, her eyes had been perpetually open and her mouth in constant motion. She was not about to miss a single event for something as worthless as sleep.

We went through the formalities of disembarking, and then proceeded to the rental car agencies, intent on renting a car to go to the hotel.

Bob began to fill out the necessary forms.

"Could I see your driver's license, please, sir?" the agent asked most respectfully. Bob obliged, by digging out his old New Mexico license.

"I'm sorry sir, but this license has expired. We have to see a valid one."

The agent handed to card back with a "what-are-you-going-to-do-now" expression on her face.

It was then that we realized that while we had been out of circulation for a year, his New Mexico license, obtained three years ago, had expired. Mine was from Iowa because I had never obtained one in the nine months I had been in New Mexico. It was still good for two months, so I handed it to the agent. She gave us a brief smile that rapidly turned to puzzlement.

"Oh. Yours is from Iowa. Is that where you live? I have family in Sioux City." She started to fill out the paperwork, asking Bob for the information necessary.

"Address?"

"Togiak, Akaska."

"Alaska? I thought you lived in Iowa."

"Nope. Alaska."

"Well, what is your address?" A forced smile

etched itself on her face.

"Togiak, Alaska."

"No, sir, I mean your street address.

"That's it. Togiak, Alaska."

Her eyes narrowed.

"You mean you have no street address?

"Yep. That's exactly what I mean. There are no streets."

I could see her waging a valiant battle with her facial nerves. The demeanor remained impassive but the voice betrayed a little frustration. She did her best to sound cheerful.

"Well okay then, how about a phone number?

"Nope. No phone."

She bit her pen and frowned. Then a light dawned and she smiled as though she had found the answer to the $64,000 question

"Then I'm sure you have a work address."

"Togiak, Alaska. And no phone there either."

She looked so pathetically at a loss that Bob took pity and figured she deserved an explanation.

"There isn't a phone in the whole town. We don't need a license because there are no roads or cars or police in the whole place."

He paused with obvious fatigue, then, with visible effort continued.

"Is all this really necessary? We just want to get to a hotel before two in the morning."

"Well, sir, we have to have some kind of record." She tried to assemble her thoughts and took a deep breath.

"You have different licenses from each other and neither of you has a valid license for the state you supposedly reside in at the moment. You don't have an address, a phone, or a work address or phone."

She shook her head in desperation.

"I'm sorry, Sir, but I'm going to have to call in my boss."

With an indignant rustle of forms, she turned and disappeared behind a door.

We looked at each other, depression setting in. Judy had sat down under the counter and was dozing.

After a couple of minutes, our interrogator returned, her superior in tow. The latter's expression indicated that she could clear up the misunderstanding in two shakes.

"Well, now, my assistant says there are a few problems here, but I'm sure that we can clear all this up when you use your credit card..."

She stopped in mid-sentence. Bob's expression had alarmed her. His tone had become menacing, his words slow and deliberate as if he was dealing with a small child.

"We don't HAVE any credit cards. We've never NEEDED any credit cards because we always pay CASH for everything, and, mostly, we don't WANT any credit cards. We don't BELIEVE in them. I realize it's un-American but the last time I looked, it wasn't a crime..."

But the agent looked at us as if we had indeed committed a crime.

"But sir, we have to have some kind of guarantee before we can let our vehicle go."

It was getting very late and we wondered if we'd find a motel room. We explained that we were prepared to write a check or even to leave a cash-security deposit. All we wanted to do was get to a hotel and drive to some car dealerships the next day.

She pursed her lips and frowned at us.

"I'm sorry sir, but there is just no way I can release a car with such sketchy information to go by."

Bob rather loudly insisted that we could leave money and checks to cover the cost of the car itself. This was only a slight exaggeration, but it was loud enough to bring Judy out from under the counter.

The two agents looked at her, looked at us, and then wanted to know if this was our "little girl."

It would indeed have taken a long stretch of the imagination to see a genetic connection. We said no but we really didn't see how that concerned them.

They looked at each other, pursed their lips in unison, and looked at us again as if we should be wearing straitjackets. They were very sorry but they couldn't help us. If we hurried, we might be able to catch the last bus into the city.

With that, they suddenly had a great need to tend to paperwork.

We stood there for a few moments, totally frustrated. Bob made some caustic reference to their "trying harder" slogan and what they could do with it. We grabbed our bags and headed for the bus stop.

Welcome to civilization. We had returned to the real world.

*   *   *

The car dealerships didn't have the hang up about credit cards that the rental agency had, so we found and paid for a small station wagon and headed down the highway toward New Mexico where we planned on staying with our friends. We camped out along the way and made good time.

All the while, Judy was getting an intense education. She was so prepared for the unexpected that if people had got around on magic carpets, she would not have been surprised.

We took her to amusement parks, to shopping malls, to museums, and to all sorts of restaurants. She went horseback riding in New Mexico, to the zoo in Chicago, and to the beaches in Massachusetts. I kept a photographic record for her of everything she did. Her mind was always working and I was made acutely aware of that one night when I heard her crying in bed. We had been explaining village life to a couple of friends at their place in New Mexico. I went to her bedroom to see what was troubling her.

After trying for an hour to find out, she finally explained that she had heard us talking about the village life and how we judged it. The other people's reactions during the conversation in question showed that they found that way of life so backwards and sometimes revolting. She was having an extremely difficult time fitting everything together and keeping things in perspective.

I felt abjectly guilty for her feelings and did my best to calm her down. For the first time, I became aware of an intense foreboding that maybe we had made an unwitting, yet grave mistake in taking her "outside" with us.

Thereafter, we made sure that all conversations with acquaintances about our experiences carried no negative overtones.

PART II

⌘

TANANA AND THE YUKON

⌘   THE GREAT INTERIOR   ⌘

Though summer was upon them, the tall Aspen shivered as the wind brushed them gently, a subtle warning of the approaching autumn. Leaves, still green, firmly clinging to silver branches, were signs of a few more months of warmth and brilliant sunlight. Later, bitten by early seasonal frost, these leaves would become the golden glory of the landscape. The wind would tear them off in a floating and rustling cascade, creating a bright yellow mantle over the hillsides, streams, and rushing rivers.

A territorial moose, feeling the strong tug of the rut, snorted and pawed at the earth, preparing himself for the possibilities of the impending mating season. As he stood in a large clearing, reflected in the dark waters of a small lake, surveying his lush kingdom, he faced the uncertainty of the season in which he was to sire generations. Breaking into a characteristic trot, the torn velvet, hanging in shreds from his new growth of antlers, and swinging in time with his loping gait, he waded into the lake to feed on the bottom growth. In a few weeks, his mating instincts would be in full bloom; he would not be wasting any time on food.

Food, on the other hand, was the primary concern of the brown bear as she added to her daily intake of thousands of calories. Two spring cubs in tow, she foraged for the nourishment that would sustain her throughout six months of near uninterrupted sleep, and a new pregnancy. As she lumbered through the undergrowth, a slight breeze ruffled her fur, highlighted by the late summer sun. Thanks to her thick layer of summer fat, the motion caused her pelt to roll gently back and forth over her massive shoulders.

Not far away, and having food as a constant concern, a lone wolf stalked a wily arctic hare. Having been cast out by his pack, he subsisted on the leavings of others. If luck favored him, he might take down a moose calf, providing the mother was distracted. That was not, however, a likely event.

This summer season had not been particularly gratifying. He carried the marks of many fights with wolves from his own pack and others, all testimony of his low rank. A torn ear, a crooked leg, a collection of jagged scars where his fur had not grown back properly, all contributed to the disrespect he encountered. His furtive gait and hanging head did not help his social standing. Perhaps, one day, he would emerge the victor in a conflict. But for now, even the wind was against him. It had changed direction so he was now upwind from the hare. The latter did not need an invitation to escape. Two hops and she was home, deep in the welcoming darkness of her burrow.

The wolf sniffed in disappointment, hoping to catch a clue of something that might represent hope in his never-ending search for food. Instead, his quivering nostrils were assailed by a disturbing and unknown scent. Curiosity driving him on, he trotted to a small rise on the hillside to see the cause of the mystery.

THE YUKON

Spring breakup on the Yukon -TANANA- 1971

Try roasting these ribs in your oven!

❧ CHAPTER 1 ❧

SANTA'S HOMETOWN

Our trip "outside" or down to "the lower 48" as Alaskans called the rest of the country, was coming to an end. Soon we'd have to make that long drive back up the ALCAN. We had to be back in Fairbanks to begin classes toward our Masters Degrees at the University. When that was over, it would be time to show up at our new station, Tanana, to begin the new school year.

We weren't absolutely sure how we were going to get there yet.

Nor did we know much about Tanana except that it was an Athapascan Indian village of about four hundred people. It had an airport, a hospital, a White Alice early warning site, two stores, a post office, and a twelve-grade school; altogether a huge and busy place compared to our last station.

We planned to arrive a few days before classes began, but, until then, we had what was left of a wild and wooly Fairbanks summer to look forward to. We had made arrangements with a teacher friend to rent her apartment in a suburb of Fairbanks called North Pole, home, naturally, of one Santa Claus. In the immediate future, the ALCAN loomed long and tedious.

It hadn't changed much in a year.

Maybe there were a few more paved miles and slightly fewer potholes, but we still felt as though we had been thrown in a blender with the switch set on "purée."

At mile zero of the highway, Dawson Creek, we stopped for lunch. Chinese food I think.

Back on the road, a few miles out of town, Judy said she didn't feel well. We told her to lie down. A few more miles and she became more vehement about it.

Finally, she screamed that she was going to throw up.

Bob veered to the shoulder of the road, leaving half the life of our tires in the gravel. We opened the door just in time for lunch to decorate the scenery. When we thought it was over, we hit the road again.

There were three repeat performances before we had gone fifteen miles, so we decided to call it a day and made camp.

The rest of the trip took on a rather subdued flavor. Whether it was our imminent parting of ways or fatigue after six weeks of travel, we'll never know.

In Fairbanks, we put Judy, her new clothes, newfound education, and souvenirs on a plane for Anchorage where someone was to help her make her connections to Dillingham and home, Togiak.

It took several weeks for things to seem normal without her. We missed her chatter, her intelligence, and her unabated interest in everything. She had left these memories with us, but we knew a part of us had gone back with her to Togiak, too.

* * *

The rest of the summer gave us time to play in the midnight sun. It was the only period of semi-decadence in our lives. Using our two-room apartment in North Pole, home of the Santa Claus House (tourist shop), as base, we went to class by day, and tried out all the entertainment spots by night. We especially enjoyed a Western style nightspot located just outside of Fairbanks, and close to home.

Some nights we'd dance and socialize until three or four in the morning, and then head for an all-night restaurant for breakfast before class. If it was a weekend, we go home and try to sleep in broad daylight even at three A.M. People didn't seem to sleep much in the constant daylight. We figured that it must do something to your chemical balance and change your sleep cycle.

Alaska's economy was on the upswing; Fairbanks had begun to experience growing pains. Trailer parks dotted areas that only last summer had been weed-strewn vacant lots. Some people were making great amounts of money. It wasn't uncommon to see hundred-dollar bills flashed in rapid succession in any place of business. New shopping centers opened, and tourist trade was brisk.

We just sat back and watched it all, missing opportunities to gamble our earnings on "sure thing" investments. Our vision was limited and we hadn't learned to think big in Alaskan terms.

Nothing wrong with our hindsight though.

We have accurate recall of every potential deal for fortune and fame that we blithely ignored; every missed opportunity for great wealth and security; every chance to "make good" on a deal.

What financial wimps we were.

*   *   *

Summer school having drawn to a close, it was time for us to rid ourselves of worldly trappings such as the car and the apartment. Our search for a buyer coincided with our search for a riverboat and motor. The plan—no room for contingency—was to pile all our belongings in the boat and point it down the Chena River that flowed into the Tanana River. We knew that by staying on that one, we'd have to eventually pass by the village of Tanana since it was down river a couple hundred miles or so.

We found a buyer for the car and a seller for the boat and motor. We said good-bye to North Pole and the Santa Claus House, and consolidated our stuff in order to make the most compact load possible.

Our new mode of transportation was a smallish green riverboat about sixteen feet long and five feet wide. It had an Evinrude 35 horsepower outboard motor of some age bolted to the stern. Actually, we didn't need the Queen Mary, as all we had was our clothing, camping and hunting gear, and the kitchenware we had used in the apartment. If you didn't count what we had stored at Bob's folks', that was pretty much the sum total of all our worldly belongings. All of it would probably fit in the boat with several square feet to spare.

At this point, we weren't worried about food for the year because we were planning on ordering our supply of it from a wholesale order catalog when we got to our new home. It would be shipped by mail from Fairbanks.

So, we were traveling very light.

On the Chena River-Getting ready to go down river to TANANA-Late summer 1970

❧ CHAPTER 2 ❧

HIGH WATER AND LOW SPIRITS

The late afternoon at the end of August found us loading the boat with everything plus several tanks of gas and an airplane map. After we sold the car, we tried again to rent one to get us around town for last-minute errands. This time we had no problem with getting the car because people seemed to be more understanding about peculiar situations up there. Now the only problem was that we had to return it to the airport, ten miles from the riverbank, back down the road. Even in Alaska, rental companies did insist that you return their vehicles.

A taxi was out of the question. There had to be a cheaper way.

In a straight line through the woods, the airport was only about three miles away. The option we chose was to have Bob return the car and then hike back to the river via a shortcut through the woods.

Meanwhile, down on the riverbank of the Chena River, I stood guard over our unprepossessing possessions.

By the time Bob showed up after his little trek through the woods, it was getting late. We figured on making it as far as the last town on the road system, Nenana, before nightfall—a term loosely applied, of course, in the midnight sun.

After Nenana, it would be total wilderness, the boat, and us.

We made the test run without incident. By ten o'clock we had secured our boat and set up our tent on the muddy bank below the only bridge leading out of Nenana back to Fairbanks.

It was our last chance to reconsider if we were inclined to.

We weren't.

The next morning, mired in mud, we took inventory of our cash. Back in Fairbanks, we hadn't planned on getting very much cash because there wouldn't have been anything to spend it on. We hadn't realized that only fifty-seven cents separated us from destitution. Desperate for a cup of hot coffee, we decided to take our chances at the local café.

A cup of coffee was fifty cents so we ordered it and shared. The owner saw us take turns at sipping it and had pity on us. He refilled the cup for nothing.

Not exactly your hearty-before-the-great-wilderness-trip breakfast.

Back in the boat we found some shredded coconut and chocolate chips left over from our cupboard in our ex-apartment. We also had a package of hot-dogs and buns, but we were saving that for lunch. We should be able to make it, without starving, to a point we figured was two thirds of the way to Tanana at a place called Manley Hot Springs.

We fired up the motor and settled in for a smooth ride down river.

The scenery was incredible, each bend in the river revealing some new beauty. In spite of it still being August, the trees were already beginning to turn slightly; the nights had already become brisk. We noticed that the river was running pretty high because there wasn't much cut bank above the water level.

We learned to avoid the treacherous "preachers:" trees buried in the river bed and protruding slightly above water, bobbing up and down as if they were a person bent over in prayer, hence the name. Often, they were hardly noticeable but deadly when run into. The "sweepers," trees growing out of the cut bank but bent over and dragging in the current, were also dangerous and to be given wide berth. Accumulating experience, we constantly scanned the river to avoid these pitfalls.

Eventually we saw something different moving in the middle of the water. We sped up to look at it and discovered that it was a black bear, swimming to the other side of the river, struggling with the current.

We watched him for a few minutes but didn't want to scare him needlessly, so we moved on in search of a good sand bar or bank for a lunch stop. We found a place where the bank was very gradual, almost like a beach. We stopped, unloaded our hotdogs, and gathered some driftwood for a small fire. We cut some willow branches to make roasting sticks.

From examining the airplane map, we could see that we were about halfway to Manley.

After our small but satisfying meal, it was hard to keep from lying in the sun and taking a nap. If it hadn't been for my constant fear of meeting a bear, we very well might have slept the afternoon away. As it was, I kept hearing suspicious noises in the undergrowth and that kept us on task.

We clambered back aboard our skiff.

After a dozen pulls on the starting rope, the engine very reluctantly sputtered to life. We looked at each other because this was not a good sign. I'm sure the used-boat salesman can be just as crooked as the proverbial used-car salesman, but a mechanical failure in this situation carried much greater implications than it would on a highway somewhere in civilization. I didn't see any freeway call boxes on the trees.

The engine ran roughly, probably on only one of its cylinders. Our progress was slower, but at least it was steady. The river widened and narrowed, became shallow in some spots. We ran aground several times. We hadn't figured out that by sticking to the gradual, beach-like bank of the river, we often didn't have enough depth to navigate.

After having struggled a half-dozen times to keep the boat afloat, we decided that a better course of action would be to stick to the "cut bank" side where the water level was lower than the bank because the action of the rushing water "cut" right into it. The water was deeper there and the current certainly seemed swifter.

Little did we know that there was much more to this than going merrily down the stream. Lives were lost every year even with experienced people who'd been navigating for years. Our ignorance of these salient facts kept us from worrying too much as we nursed the ailing engine for mile after mile of lonely country. I'd check our progress by comparing landmarks to the topographical markings of the airplane map.

"There's really nowhere we can go wrong," we thought naively, because there were no tributaries to be mistaken for the main branch.

At one point, we knew that the Yukon River would merge with the Tanana, but that was just before we arrived at the village, and we'd take care of that when we got there, probably tomorrow morning.

We decided to keep the motor running as long as possible without making any kind of pit stops. Stopping and starting was asking for mechanical trouble.

We didn't exactly have to worry about privacy and learned to balance ourselves on the edge of the boat for a kind of mobile pit stop when natural urges dictated.

Even so, I couldn't help feeling that the forest had eyes and took care of business as furtively as possible.

In that position, you feel incredibly vulnerable, especially when the driver, itchy finger on the throttle, has no respect, and a very dubious sense of humor.

*   *   *

By nine o'clock we were still short of our destination and began to look for some sort of reference point that would help us find Manley.

Soon, on the north bank we could see a small opening that turned out to be a little slough. We followed it slowly, admiring its almost fairy-tale-like qualities.

The water was glassy, blanketed by patches of some kind of surface algae.   The banks, so close together, met each other with their intertwined trees forming a natural canopy.   The late sun filtered through the branches and dappled the water with its slanted rays. The soft light, the silence, and the warmth of the sun's rays bathed us in a magical calm and lethargy.

We completely lost track of time.

The charm of the spot however, could not suppress the attack hunger was waging. In our minds' eyes, the leftover hotdogs tucked away somewhere in the recesses of our mountain of gear were taking on the proportions of a major feast.

Nudging the boat further upstream, we came to an opening complete with gravel beach and dock. We felt as though we had landed in a remote little chunk of Switzerland.

We tied up at the dock, grabbed our camping gear,

and trudged across the surprisingly attractively landscaped property.

Set in a large clearing, with a backdrop of forested hillside, the Manley Lodge presented an inviting picture. Someone had taken a lot of trouble to cultivate a profusion of flowers and plants and had arranged them all to their best advantage. The whole place felt totally in keeping with the magical quality of the slough. Whoever lived here had it made. There were some outbuildings, a vegetable garden, an airplane hangar with accompanying tool shop, and a complete riverboat set-up.

We decided to camp alongside the slough but in view of the lodge. It gave me a comfortable feeling to see a bona fide housing structure.

Soon we were salivating at the aroma of hotdogs sizzling on the end of yet another willow branch. If we'd had any money, we'd have sauntered over to the lodge to see if they had had anything better, but having no idea what kind of a business was operated there, we were afraid to invade anyone's privacy. We knew that the hot springs were a drawing card for whatever tourist might venture this far into the wilderness, but we weren't sure if reservations were in order or not. And we knew we didn't exactly look like a couple out of the L.L. Bean catalog. At any rate, the place looked deserted at the moment. The owners were probably away or something.

After thinking in these terms and settling down to a restful night under the tent, it was disconcerting to be violently awakened by music from the lodge blaring into the night. Our grogginess led us to believe for a moment that we were back in the city. Someone was having a party and didn't mind disturbing the whole countryside.

Oh well, how long could it last anyway? We'd eventually get some sleep when the partiers saw the wisdom of doing the same.

Giving up on sleep for a while, we left the tent for a walk by the water and noticed that the sun must have gone back to setting at least a little, since there was a duskiness to the light now, and shadows were indistinct.

We returned to the tent in the foolish hope that the music would quit.

It didn't.

By four o'clock, we should have understood the effect of unending daylight on people's sleep cycles in the bush: you simply sleep whenever there isn't something better to do. If you miss out on some sleep, you can easily make up for it when the darkness of winter hits.

Not being educated in this, we didn't know we were being exposed to the rule rather than the exception.

*   *   *

To say that we emerged bleary-eyed from our so-called rest spot a few hours later is to understate the situation. We forced ourselves to gather the gear together and drag everything down to the boat.

Estimating the distance to our destination at about sixty miles, we didn't do a particularly neat job of securing everything. We had left Fairbanks a day later than expected and realized that our friends in Tanana were expecting us by now. We didn't want to be the cause for an expensive search and rescue expedition they would launch if we didn't get there soon.

The boat motor registered its balky nature right from the start. It took dozens of pulls and spark plug cleaning before it finally sputtered half-heartedly to life. Not often in our prayers, the person who had sold us the motor must have felt his ears burning because that's what we felt like doing to him. There has to be a special place in the hereafter for people who sold lemons to unsuspecting customers.

Not five miles down river, the lemon quit altogether and could not be resurrected in spite of Bob's valiant, if not panic-stricken efforts.

As he tore the engine cover off and tried as many tricks as his limited experience would allow, the boat rotated dizzyingly end to end, in a circular pattern, caught by the swift current. I tried my best to ward off the "preachers" and "sweepers" who would have caused us untold distress if allowed to get us in their "clutches." If they managed to capsize the boat, we'd lose everything we owned, not to mention our lives.

At one point the river widened, slowing the current. We didn't know whether to hope to be grounded or to keep using the current to our advantage. In any case, it ended up not being up to us. We came to a sudden jarring halt. Almost thrown overboard by the shock, Bob grabbed the side of the boat and avoided a sudden bath.

"It's another damned sandbar."

Cursing our luck, we pulled on our hip boots and were about to push the boat to deeper water when we noticed a twelve-foot long two-by-four, lying not three yards away, as though sent by Providence. Not knowing exactly how it would help us, Bob nevertheless dug it out of the muddy gravel and dumped it across our pile of stuff. It reached from prow to stern.

After about ten to fifteen minutes of pushing and pulling the boat, we were free of the sandbar. Gratefully and breathlessly we pulled ourselves in over the sides of the boat.

We couldn't afford the luxury of catching our breath lest we run aground again. Constant vigilance was the order of the day.

Bob picked up the two-by-four, not realizing it marked the beginning of a beautiful relationship. The giant piece of wood was perfect to fend off danger. He could use it to keep the uprooted timber and the floating logs out of the way. It helped avoid the sandbars and served as a makeshift, albeit clumsy, paddle.

From the stern, Bob would push and row once or twice on one side, yell "Fore," at which time I'd duck. Then he'd swing the dripping twelve feet of wood over to the other side to push and row there. This proved effective in keeping the prow of the boat pointed downstream, a vast improvement over the end-to-end locomotion of before.

It also thoroughly wet everything inside the boat.

I tried to figure out a way I could help because I

knew that that kind of rowing was very tiring. Bob's strength was the only thing between us and total disaster. I had to figure out a way to conserve it.

In a moment of brilliance, I extricated my prize Teflon-coated frying pan from the pile of largely damp possessions now spread in complete disarray at the bottom of the boat, and plunged it, canoe-paddle style, into the river.

We now had prototypes of both the world's longest and shortest paddles. We might have looked mad, but there was certainly method in our actions. We could have gone on for miles, I suppose, as long as I remembered to duck at the appropriate time.

Just a question of timing.

Than it proved to be a question of muscle-power and fatigue. Every time we relaxed or lost concentration, the boat would begin its crazy rotation and risk capsizing when we'd be dragged along sideways.

We knew had to make plans for an eventual landing. I left the navigation to Bob while I consulted the airplane map.

A fact of no particular impact as long as we had had power, was the existence of a long island in the middle of the river, immediately across from Tanana. By looking at the map, I realized that if we passed Tanana on the south side of the island instead of the north, it would obscure the village and we'd completely miss it.

That would also mean we'd then be downstream of it.

Floating downstream even under difficult circumstances doesn't begin to complicate matters as does trying to go upstream to get somewhere. I knew that getting caught in that trap could turn a salvageable situation like ours into a desperate one. Adding to the picture was the confluence, at one point, of our river, the Tanana, with the mighty Yukon.

Who knew what goes on at the merging of two swiftly moving rivers when you have to get from the south bank of the lower one to the north bank of the upper one, powered only by two sets of biceps?

Although we couldn't see it, we knew that the Yukon was running virtually parallel with us by now, about ten or so miles directly north.

There was no alternative but to fight the current and get from the south bank to the north bank of "our" river. Once there, we could paddle our way up a little channel that occurred at the merging "our" river with the Yukon. From there, we hoped we could force ourselves across the Yukon from its south bank to the north bank and end up on the correct side of it so as not to miss the village.

So, to recap, all we had to do was fight two currents in two major swiftly running rivers, plus a channel, in a very short distance, with a two-by-four and a frying pan to serve as oars.

Then we'd be fine.

I told Bob that if we reached that point, after I had kissed the ground, I would walk to Tanana, no matter how far it might be.

I didn't get much argument.

From the map, I knew that we should soon be able to see the White Alice Early Warning Site, located eight miles above Tanana.

We began paddling in quiet desperation, willing the boat to the opposite bank. Soon we could see the domed buildings of the site and knew that the moment of truth had indeed arrived. The opening to the channel should be around the next bend.

That the river had widened proved to be a mixed blessing. Yes, it made the distance longer, but it was also shallower, enabling Bob to get good pushes off the bottom with his pole.

Our silent relief at reaching the north bank of the Tanana turned to horror as we felt the power of the current. The rough action of the water was causing huge chunks of the cut bank to slough into the river. The periodic "plop" startled us every time. By hugging the bank we risked being swamped by one of these, but if we didn't stay close, we'd never have the strength to cover the longer distance to the channel.

As we absolutely had to get to the channel for access to the Yukon, we had no choice but to stay next to the cut bank despite its dangers.

The channel, it turned out, gave us an unexpected chance to rest and to meet some of our future fellow-residents. The north bank receded we approached the channel and we were surprised to find calmer, eddying water in it.

Catching our breath and resting our arms we stared stupidly into the distance.

Were our ears deceiving us, or was that really the noise of an engine? In our exhausted stupor, we couldn't be sure.

Straining our eyes, we gradually focused on a boat making its way in our direction.

Embarrassed, we hid our "paddles" and just sat there, dumb, as though all was normal. Two villagers smiled and waved from their boat, showing no inclination to stop on their way upstream.

Suddenly, we woke up at the same time.

"Where's Tanana?" we shouted in their direction as if we were just on a Sunday outing.

They pointed vaguely in the direction we had guessed at. We heard something about "...not too far..." as they continued upstream.

One of those relative terms again.

By this time, lactic acid was taking permanent residence in my arms and back. If the Yukon was swifter than the Tanana had been, I had serious doubts about succeeding in our quest.

The boat barely moving, Bob rested on his pole while I tried to massage away some of the soreness in my neck. I didn't want to look at my hands that I knew were rubbed raw from gripping my "oar" with constantly wet skin.

We were both so thirsty that we scooped up a mouthful or two of murky river water.

No matter how we procrastinated, we knew the

next efforts were unavoidable.

"Might as well get this over with," Bob grunted with all the enthusiasm of someone going in for a root canal.

I dared to hope that before the fight with nature began, some charitable soul would happen by and tow us, but no one was in sight either up river or down. It was us (no need to be grammatical...) against the world again.

As we rowed our way through the calmer water of the channel, we could hear the rush of the Yukon water. As we neared the river itself, we felt more and more turbulence. The north bank of the Tanana was now also the south bank of the Yukon that came to a "v" jutting into the channel. Once we passed the "v," we had our first look eastward at the river of historical fame. What immediately struck us was that it was so much neater than the Tanana. The north bank was smooth gravel and heavily wooded. There didn't seem to be as many trees and logs in the water, and there weren't the shallow spots with their accompanying sandbars.

There was, however, a very healthy current that immediately grabbed us and almost flipped the boat.

Fighting soreness and fatigue, we tried to steady ourselves and paddle toward the north bank. Luckily, a section of the north bank looking like a small spit of land protruded into the river, giving us a better angle to shoot for.

The frying pan and the two-by-four flashed into action again and again. Somehow we found renewed vigor at the prospect of almost having reached our goal.

The river was too deep for Bob to reach the bottom, so he had to wield the twelve-foot oar with special skill from side to side. He tried holding it in different places and at different angles, but if the truth were told, it would be said that, this time, my short, stubby frying pan was making more progress. If it held out through the ordeal, I was going to write a "satisfied consumer" letter to the manufacturer. This was way above the call of duty for something that was only supposed to fry bacon and eggs for breakfast.

Whether it was thanks to the plank or the pan, a few aching minutes later, we grated to a stop on the north bank of the Yukon.

We sat in what can only be described as a catatonic trance. The silence was broken by the gentle tinkling of the glacial silt along the bottom of the boat and a little grinding as the current silently, but insistently, dragged the bow of the boat along the gravel beach. We didn't even have the energy to clamber out and push the boat higher to safety.

We still weren't sure of how far we were from the village and mentally prepared ourselves for a hike of indeterminate distance. Our stuff, now soaking in an inch or so of water, would have to wait in the boat until we could get back to it.

As we tried to gird ourselves for renewed effort, a new noise made its way into our consciousness: a motor coming downstream toward us.

I guess natural defense against insanity allowed us to ignore the irony of being rescued after our struggle instead of before.

The pilot of the boat, a white man, drew up alongside us and, seeing what must have been the two most exhausted faces he had ever laid eyes on, he asked if we were all right. We explained our situation and he exclaimed, "Oh, you're the guys everyone was wondering about. They were expecting you yesterday and were hoping you hadn't drowned or something. Did you know, with all the rain we've had, the river's really bad this year? How about a tow into town?"

We must have looked pathetically happy in a dazed kind of way.

If we had been able to think clearly, the irony of rounding the bend and running smack into the village would not have escaped us. We hadn't even been a mile from our destination. As it was, we were too tired, hungry, dirty, and not a little embarrassed. Some villagers were walking along the bank, putting things in their boats and stacking fishing gear. One or two looked up at us in mild interest and went back to their work.

The new teachers had arrived. Not exactly in style, but we had arrived.

❧ CHAPTER 3 ❧

ON THE BANKS OF THE YUKON

It was a metropolis compared to our last place of residence. A post office, Northern Commercial store, fifteen-bed-hospital, hospital compound, FAA station with accompanying airport, and twelve room school all graced the top of the high riverbank, overlooking the half mile wide river.

Not able to face the prospect of carrying our gear around, we left everything in the boat and trudged up the bank. School didn't start for another week but we had a lot of settling in to do before we could even think of the job.

Upon finding our friends who lived in the teacher apartment attached to the school, we discovered that there was no housing for us at this time.

Where had we heard that before?

For tonight, we'd have to be satisfied with camping out in the school office. At this point in our lives, anything short of spending the night in the boat was acceptable. We could have slept soundly on a bed of nails if we'd had to.

After a welcome meal of black-bear roast and home baked bread, we stumbled through the school hallway in the dark, not knowing where the master light switch was. We found the office door, opened it, and dumped our sleeping bags on the first open floor space we found. It took us all of a minute and a half to strip off our damp, grimy travelling clothes and gratefully pass out.

The night proved way too short.

At six o'clock, we were wrenched from exhausted sleep by the pounding of hammers and the screeching of a power saw. We forced our eyelids apart to find that we had been lying right next to a glass partition, in plain view of a dozen men working on the school. Our state of undress indicated that we had been counting on privacy, and I thought I caught some surreptitious smiles going by. We dressed inside our sleeping bag and emerged sheepishly in search of some kind of breakfast.

* * *

The next few days saw us move into a thirty-year-old house on the main street, previously inhabited by a church minister. There was electricity but no running water. The house had been plumbed for some kind of drainage however, because we could use the drains in the

157

sink and toilet. A bucket of water served as the flusher for the toilet and a rinser for the sink.

The house was handily located right across the street from the community well house, so, in a way, we did have running water. All we had to do was string a hundred-foot hose through the living area, the hallway, the little yard with a picket fence in front, across the street to the well house, and turn on the pump.

Presto.

Water gushed out the other end into whatever we had that could contain it. We invested in two huge plastic garbage cans to serve as holding tanks, thus reducing our need to string the hose every day. We quickly learned to use the minimum amount of water for our everyday activities. We could brush our teeth with three tablespoons of it and wash dishes with a few cups full. Extensive bathing however, we took care of by borrowing the shower in one of the teaching couple's trailers. Every Sunday we'd roll our clean underwear in a towel and traipse over to take advantage of the kind shower offer.

*   *   *

Lack of water was not the only element we had to deal with. Fire was the other one, because here was the little matter of heating the house. The only way to heat the very drafty house was with the wood stove located in the main living area. It took a few days to learn its many idiosyncrasies.

One of the basic requirements was fuel. Outside the back of the house we saw a supply of logs that we assumed were for our use. So as to reduce his workload, Bob was quick to teach me the art of log splitting. If he hadn't made so much fun of my novice attempts, I probably would have been more favorably disposed towards it. At any rate, the wood I chopped kept us just as warm as his geometrically accurate chunks, so, after a decent interval, he dispensed with the unappreciated humor.

Fuel for the fire! TANANA - Fall - 1970

We thought we had mastered the whole heater idea until we woke up one night coughing and choking in thick acrid smoke. It took us the rest of the night to correct the flue and the intake vent and to air out the house. By six, the house was relatively clear but it was also about forty degrees. We recognized that it was better to be cold and able to breathe, than warm and suffocating. School dragged on interminably that day, and we made sure to fine-tune the stove before going to bed that evening.

Another morning arrived prematurely in our little house. We awoke to the repeated thud of someone chopping wood.

Misanthrope that he was, Bob jumped up and yelled something about getting the thief who was robbing us of our precious fuel supply.

We both dashed to the back door to find old man Willie chopping away, splitting logs. In answer to our unvoiced question he explained that he was doing this for us because we worked hard teaching his grandchildren, and we deserved a rest.

Although our panic had not been entirely uncalled for, we nevertheless felt acutely embarrassed at this show of genuine kindness. We thanked him profusely as he continued to work, and went back to bed.

Burying our heads in our pillows, we just wished he could do it at a later hour.

Because we were sort of temporarily established in a house not really ours, we couldn't do the things to the house that it badly needed. From the floor to the ceiling, from the pipes to the wiring, from the outside to the inside, working on it could have kept us busy all year. Just caulking all the leaks in the walls could have been a full-time occupation. Instead, we just tried to ignore the shortcomings. When the wind whistled noisily through the myriad of cracks, we just turned up the stereo. When we used the makeshift toilet, we got good at holding our breath so as not to gag on the smell of constipated plumbing. When the wind blew the smoke down the stack back into our living room, we went outside for a breath of clean air.

You can get used to just about anything if you have to.

House on Main Street, Tanana.

For entertainment, we had to resort to the old fishing and hunting routine. After thinking that we'd never feel like climbing aboard the boat again, it was only a matter of time before we felt the need to explore the environment and maybe harvest some meat at the same time.

On the advice of local people, we invested in a so-called jet motor: an outboard motor that operated on a jet of water instead of a propeller. It sucked up water and spewed it out the back, illustrating the old equal and opposite reaction principle. This enabled us to travel in small shallow streams without the worry of grinding a propeller in the gravel.

On a trip down river, we spotted a large moose trudging along one of the sandy banks. We weren't seriously hunting but were nevertheless interested in the large beast, as we hadn't yet seen that many at close range. He began to lope up the beach in order to avoid us. Bob nosed the boat as close as he dared so as not to ground us. We'd had enough of that on our original trip.

Close enough to hear the moose grunt, we could see saliva dripping from his large velvety mouth. One of his brow tines was broken, and one of his ears was split.

He turned to watch us with a crazy eyeball. I half expected him to wheel and charge. He had obviously been in one hell of a fight.

"I hope he's tired out from it," I thought fervently to myself, not wanting to be his next sparring partner.

I was just about to suggest that Bob stop the pursuit when there was a sudden shock to the boat. We knew we had hit something--probably a loose rock.

Our speed was reduced to practically nothing although the revolutions of the engine remained constant. It was as if a giant hand was holding the boat back. We were now barely advancing against the current.

The moose gave us one last disdainful look as he loped off through the trees. It was as if he knew we were no menace to him.

It got later and later and still we barely crept along, heading for home. Normal propulsion would have had us there, drinking a hot-buttered rum by a warm stove, hours ago.

Finally it was so dark and cold that Bob half-heartedly suggested that we stop somewhere along the bank to spend the night. When he saw the look on my face, he reconsidered. My ever-present fear of bears provided the necessary motivation to keep us inching up the river.

*   *   *

An interesting optical illusion kept me mesmerized and helped make the time go by. When I looked up at the spruce trees lining the bank high above us, I found that the second row, barely outlined against the deepening sky, seemed to be slowly trudging past the first row in the same direction we were. The spiky and irregularly shaped spruce trees looked like huge, dark, hooded giants eerily marching in a macabre funeral procession up the river. Thereafter, I couldn't help watching this phenomenon on any number of late excursions, and, although I knew it was just an illusion, it never ceased to give me an uneasy feeling.

Jarred back to reality by the cold and fatigue, I was happy to find that, inch by slow inch, we were finally rounding the last bend before the village.

*   *   *

After a third eternity, we made it home.

Once on the firm ground, an examination of the jet motor revealed that the rock we had hit had knocked the reverse cup partially over the jet opening, thereby reducing the power to almost nothing.

Another wet, cold, and needlessly long exercise in futility to add to our repertoire of the same.

Seeing the moose up close and personal however, had softened the edges a bit.

☙ CHAPTER 4 ❧

IT'S ALL IN THE ACT

The job situation was vastly different from Togiak that now seemed a hundred years away. In the first place, teaching teenagers is a whole different story, and although they tend to respond in similar ways to teenagers anywhere, there were some cultural influences at play.

The hardest thing for me to deal with was their reluctance to participate verbally in classroom activities. This, added to the fact that I was teaching Spanish, English and Drama, all orally oriented subjects, made things especially difficult.

Because the Athapascan Indians had always been very much a communal society for survival purposes, everyone is supposed to contribute in some way and no one is supposed to stand out either by accomplishment or standing. All things must be distributed evenly and no one should gain too much recognition. This attitude directly conflicts with the American system of education where competition and recognition are much-needed requirements for apparent success.

Oral class participation was just about nil as I started my new classes. Trying to get each student to read aloud audibly was difficult enough; to get them to stand up in front of others to act out a part was as close to impossible as anything I've ever tried in a classroom. In addition, if the students weren't on a sugar high or low, tired from being up until extremely late, or bouncing off a dire family argument, they were suffering from hangovers because someone had made a "booze order" last night in spite of the ordinance against it.

I remember, a few years later, being relieved that they had changed from drinking alcohol to smoking marijuana because at least the latter didn't cause them to pass out during a bathroom break.

After dealing with this all morning, there were many times that I couldn't get lunch down because my stomach was tied up in emotional knots. Every day I tried to come up with a different approach or to change behavior in some way so that we could get something worthwhile done in class. Eventually, as I revealed more about myself and spent a great deal of time discussing issues close to their hearts, we built a good relationship and many of the kids began to do things to please me, if for no other reason. They all tended to hide behind their self-imposed uniforms: jeans, jeans jackets, blue headbands and tennis shoes. As they slowly emerged from this denim enclave, I began to get to know them and enjoy their individualities. Later, when I had a sewing class and smock tops were in style, there came a new fashion consciousness whereby at least the girls began to vary their outfits, proud of their handmade projects.

My biggest hurdle in the first year was self-imposed and therefore not mandatory, but a point of honor I took up with myself. I wanted the drama class to put on a full-fledged three or five-act play, complete with stage, scenery and costumes. I wanted it performed for the entire community. To go from a class full of mumbling readers to stage hams in three months would be a true mark of progress.

There was very little material available in the way of play scripts and the nearest public library was in Fairbanks so I spent many frustrating hours leafing through catalogs, looking for an appropriate play.

I noticed that westerns were a big item at the local movie theater (the basement of the nurses' quarters at the hospital) so when I came across a spoof western, I knew I had found my answer. I don't recall the actual obtaining of the play but by mid-October, we were tentatively reading and trying to cast parts. I don't think there was even one student who gave the project a fighting chance, but I persisted.

A couple of the boys, having the sophistication that a year in a city school had given them, condescended to take on the meatier parts. They began to memorize. Things were going better than expected. The janitors had agreed to construct a rudimentary stage and we obtained some large pieces of corrugated cardboard for the sets.

The first setback occurred when one of the leads discovered that he was to lie in a coffin for a few of the scenes. Having just witnessed his father's death as a result of a barroom brawl in Fairbanks, and probably somewhat affected by cultural superstitions, he drew the line at this point.

Death, violent or otherwise, seemed always to stalk the village populations, yet, as common as it might be, no one was ever at ease dealing with it.

After some desperate deliberation, I was able to convince another student to switch roles with him. This student, having always shown superior knowledge of how things were "outside," thanks to several years in a boarding school, took it upon himself to rise above the situation. He was familiar with the lines of the role in question since the two parts were played opposite each other throughout the play. I don't know whether it was his extra experience or some special strength of character that enabled him to cast aside the influence of strong superstitions, but I was relieved and grateful. He earned his "A+" right there. Little did I know the impact this episode would eventually have.

The coffin in question was fashioned by one of the construction workers with whom we had formed a friendship. It had to have strong handles because the play called for the actor to be carried on to the stage in it. You could have heard the proverbial pin drop even on the carpeting the day he brought it to class. It was one of those chilling moments you remember forever. The kids stopped what they were doing and just stared. Chiding myself all the while, I felt the hairs on the back of my neck rise.

The coffin was plain pine, but in order to make it realistic, he had tapered it and made one end three sided instead of just squaring off the end. There was no mistaking it for a run-of-the-mill rectangular box. I looked at the actor who would have the closest connection to it and tried to think of something light hearted to say. He beat me to it. "I hope you made it comfortable so I can sleep through the boring parts," he joked. "Let's take a look."

The moment had passed and natural curiosity took over. Sensing the situation, the carpenter made a scientific event out of it by explaining how he had designed and built it. We tucked it unobtrusively in a corner and by that time, the bell had rung. I had a hard time getting lunch down that day too.

Enthusiasm gained on apathy. By the week of the performance, lines had been memorized, props had been assembled, and scenery had been painted depicting a typical main street of the old West, complete with swinging doors to the saloon. The student taking the part of the saloon girl must have practiced bursting out of the doors a million times. She had been one of the shyest in the class and had developed into a class "A" ham.

We had decided to place the coffin on stage rather than carry it in because the "pall bearers" didn't quite have the control needed make a smooth entrance. We had decided to present the dress rehearsal to the student body as a kind of pilot program. I noticed that the "preacher" was relying rather heavily on his Bible for his lines. Upon inquiry, I found that he had inserted little pieces of paper containing his lines between the Bible pages and in this way saved himself some homework.

The rehearsal went well and we went over the timetable for the performance. We did not have an auditorium at the time (that's one of the reasons for the new construction on the school) but we had a double classroom that had been changed into one. Every spare chair in the school, church and city hall had been brought out and put in rows for the occasion. We had planned two performances for the weekend: Friday and Saturday night. I had no idea if people would come or not. I was prepared for the ones who did come, to do it on "Indian Time" (when you felt like it; not necessarily on time) so I was taken aback when some people showed up even before the program distributors. By curtain time, every seat was filled and more.

Now I was really sweating it.

The fruits of my efforts were on the line. I was gratified by the cohesiveness of the cast and crew in getting things flowing smoothly and I think they were surprised at how much fun they were having. The audience in general was completely awed, and those who had children on stage showed obvious pride. The story couldn't have been more appropriate and everyone laughed at the right times. When the star burst out of his coffin at the key moment, the entire audience jumped in unison. Altogether it was the overwhelming success the director always wants.

After a good night's sleep, we'd be ready for a repeat performance. I knew that having to get through an entire Saturday without anyone getting into some kind of trouble was against the odds, but I dismissed my doubts. It was only when I saw my "preacher" being held up by the "sheriff" and the "saloon girl" just before curtain time that I knew I should have been more realistic in my expectations. They all looked up apologetically at me and said that they had tried cold water and coffee but nothing could sober up the "preacher" who had found some of the wrong kind of spirits. At least most of his lines were written on those pieces of paper in his Bible. If they could find the Bible, we had it under control. Luckily, the prop person had had the presence of mind to gather everything in one place. The Bible was there, it's extra verses intact.

That night, most of the audience thought that the role of the drunken preacher was played with extraordinary skill. There were only a few raised eyebrows when he stuttered and stumbled, inexplicably scattering parts of his Bible to the four winds. The other members of the cast did their best to cover the lapses in dialogue and my blood pressure didn't go a point over two hundred the whole evening. I don't think I could have taken a third show and remained sane. I was content in the knowledge that the play was a topic of conversation for years, and, unfortunately, there was never another one like it.

☙ CHAPTER 5 ❧

THE MECHANICS OF TEMPERATURE

Meanwhile, back at the wood house, we were packing our things to move into the teacher housing. Our "temporary" living arrangement had been almost a duplicate of our situation in Togiak, only a year before.

There were six new trailers lined up behind the school building, waiting to be hooked up to utilities. It took several weeks before the ditches were dug, pipe and wiring was laid, and heat tape was applied to all water and drain lines.

Sometime at the end of October we moved into a new trailer again. Carpeting was a luxury after the cracked and peeling linoleum of our little house on Main Street. We were overjoyed at being able to take a shower on any day of the week. We took nothing for granted anymore, but felt fairly secure with new plumbing, new electrical wiring, and new heating system.

As the weather grew colder, we noticed that the furnace cycled continually. Sometimes it would ignite,

173

but the fan would fail, and the whole thing would shut off. Pretty soon it began to make odd noises. We asked the maintenance people about it but, after a cursory examination, they couldn't solve anything.

The night temperature was dipping to zero, and we noticed frost patches forming on the inside of our walls. In fact, we could tell how cold it was outside by the size of the patches inside. We finally became irritated at not being able to reach a comfortable temperature, and having to wear our parkas in the living room.

Bob decided he would take matters into his own hands by examining the furnace. Not waiting for my vote, he fiddled around, and then told me to go down the hall and turn up the thermostat.

What followed was a deafening explosion and the fastest thirty-yard dash up a hallway by a white man in history.

The cold we had felt with a malfunctioning heater certainly couldn't compare to what it was like waiting for a replacement to be flown out to us. We later heard that almost every furnace in every new trailer purchased by that state all the way down the Yukon River had to be replaced. Ours did have the distinction however, of being the only one with a cracked firebox.

The others had just blown their stacks.

*   *   *

As the temperature continued its downward plunge, and the old timers muttered seeing signs that this would be the coldest winter in many, many years, we busied ourselves with everyday chores, not really paying too much attention to the thermometer.

After a major snowfall in November, we decided to take some pictures with our new camera and tripod set-up. We had bought two new snowmobiles, and were anxious to try them out too.

So we made our first trip a photographic expedition.

There were several snowmobile trails, already compacted, leading through the woods. They were actually not just for the machines, but also for the dog teams to practice on. Dog sled racing was a major activity in the interior of the state, and many of the best dogs were bred in Tanana.

There were no speed limits and no traffic to hamper the very exhilarating feeling we got from speeding through the frozen forest.

We found a likely spot to try out our camera, so we turned off the snow machines. As soon as the ringing subsided in our ears, we felt more than heard the deep silence surrounding us. As bright as the day was, and as breathtakingly beautiful as the scenery was, we felt intimidated. We knew that if the snowmobiles decided to be obnoxious, we would not be enjoying the scenery.

As soon as we walked off the compacted trail, we sank to our knees. It would be absolutely impossible to hike anywhere. I was beginning to feel the cold through my boots and two pairs of thick socks and getting a little impatient. Bob was trying to set up the tripod, but since he had to work gloveless, the process had slowed considerably. His fingers operated in slow motion.

Finally everything was ready. I struck an appropriate arctic pose and Bob pulled the tripod lever to change the angle of the camera. A sharp snap broke the white stillness, and Bob stood there with a stupid look on his face, and the camera at the end of the upraised lever in his hand. The cold had caused the metal to snap in two. The expensive tripod was now not worth the snow it was sitting on.

The trip home was less than exhilarating. I couldn't help thinking of our ex-tripod hanging high in a spruce tree like a giant Christmas ornament, courtesy of a frustrated photographer.

*　*　*

I guess the old timers had correctly interpreted the signs. The mercury crouched lower and lower in its tube. Our tripod had snapped at fifty below, and we were well past the minus sixty-mark now. We wore our parkas and Sorel boots almost every time we stepped outside. Luckily our ruffs, put together by an Eskimo lady back in Togiak, contained an outer section of wolf fur and an inner section of wolverine fur. The wolverine fur shafts were hollow and didn't freeze in spite of our condensing breath.

A walk outside prematurely aged you immediately because the condensation would freeze on your brows and lashes, giving you the "gray" look. Your nose would tickle because of the frozen hairs snapping each time you wrinkled it. Mustaches and beards were particularly at risk, often becoming totally glaciated and stuck together. At first, coming into the house after having been outside for a while, Bob always forgot to let them thaw before trying to speak. The result was severe pain from the pulled hairs followed by a stream of expletives, herein deleted.

And, there are other things you learn about cold weather gear, as one of our friends in another village discovered. He came to be known because of his one minute of concentration-loss at a time when most people concentrate very deeply.

On his way home after a long snowmobile ride one day, nature made a call that couldn't be denied even at thirty or forty (or sixty as the story gained momentum) below zero at about ten or twenty (or forty or fifty) miles from home. Fortunately for the cold aspect, but very unfortunately for the tactic about to be performed, he was wearing a full-length snowmobile suit. After a panic-stricken moment wrestling out of the top part and pulling it down to his ankles, he found an uprooted spruce tree to lean against to conduct his business. A minute or two later, much relieved but shaking with cold, he hurriedly pulled his clothes back on, zipped up his snowmobile suit, and looked to see if he had done major damage to the environment.

It soon became apparent that something was amiss because he could find no evidence of his action of a minute ago. His mystification was short lived however, as he became aware of extra warmth and weight at his back. Realization came in horrifying waves: he had failed to pull his suit enough out of the way. After pulling it back on, he had zipped the evidence right up inside it.

His trip the rest of the way home is the stuff of nightmares.

Our snow machines proved to be very moody, especially at temperatures under thirty below or so. We never went on any kind of trip without a six-pack of sparkplugs in our pockets. They seemed to foul continually. We figured that for every hour we spent driving the snowmobile, we spent two hours working on them. In addition, we noticed that our right arms were becoming disproportionally developed and decided that this phenomenon was due to having to pull on the starter rope dozens of times every time we wanted to use the snowmobiles. At the beginning, I had to use two hands to get enough friction to start the motor. After a few weeks, I was able to do an impressive and authoritative one-armed pull. This show of strength was more than simply that. It was a necessity in case no one was around to help me. I knew I'd be taking the machine on my own sometimes and would have only myself to rely on. Bob insisted that I learn the elements of a two-cycle engine for the same reason.

When things went properly, we'd take the

machines out at night for a moonlit ride in the forest. We had become skillful drivers and were able to maneuver the machines over all sorts of terrain.

The snow covered nightscape never ceased to enthrall us. The blanketed ground always reminded me of a description I must have read somewhere about a "sea of diamonds sparkling in fiery splendor." It may have been a cliché, but it was certainly an apt description of the scenery in this case.

If we didn't go cross-country, we'd race up the White Alice Site road with some of our friends.

One particular acquaintance, who always seemed to want to impress me, constantly tried to beat my machine. His had more horsepower, but mine was much lighter, giving me the edge.

His misplaced competition only served to pile him up in the ditch one night, when he was paying too much attention to passing me, and not enough on where he was headed. It doesn't take much to total a cowling made of fiberglass. You'd have thought we were a couple of kids drag racing in high school or something.

Maybe the temperature was restricting the blood flow to our brains.

∂ CHAPTER 6 ∽

WHITEOUT!

One of our longer excursions took place in fifty-below weather or colder. We started the trip with five snowmobiles and three attached sleds.

Our destination was the point at which we could catch sight of a migrating herd of Caribou. It was basically a scouting trip, which was to be followed by a real hunting expedition a few days later. Our guide for the scouting trip had lived his entire life in this area and was guaranteed to know it thoroughly.

We left the house at six in the morning one Saturday. From the way smoke took a downward turn as soon as it came out of the stacks and sidled down the chimneys, the walls, and dropped to the lowest point possible, we knew the temperature was proportionally low.

There is a scientific explanation for the smoke going down rather than rising, but we never found it out. We didn't even want to know what the exact temperature reading was. It was common practice not to find out the exact measurement because that always made you feel colder.

We prepared ourselves to ride our snowmobiles about seven miles up to the White Alice Site where we would meet the others going on the trip with us.

The "site" as it was commonly known, was part of the national early warning system set up by the government in case of attack by Russia. A staff of technicians was responsible for its operation. They were under contract by the defense department and usually signed on for a couple of years. The site itself consisted of two huge satellite dishes with sensitive radar systems, some offices and living quarters.

The thing most well known and appreciated locally about the place however, was the kitchen. The government provided an array of epicurean delights and an experienced cook who could make the most of the items at his disposal. We supposed that this was the government's way of ensuring that no one would leave before his stint was up; the great food was to make up for whatever other amenities of civilization were lacking in this wilderness outpost. It was widespread knowledge that the staff enjoyed lobster tail and steak whenever they had a yearning for them. There were significant between-meal snacks twenty-four hours a day to tide you over from one meal to the next. It was a fact that most staff members left their assignment considerably heavier then when they arrived.

I have my suspicions that the real reason Bob made friends with some of the men up there was that he has deep appreciation for good cooking and he often supplemented his daily intake with items from the perpetually laden snack table.

It took all our energy to start the snow machines. We made up our minds then and there that our next ones would have electric starts for sure. We rode the seven miles up the frozen road to the site. We had pulled our ruffs out to their maximum extent to form a little hot air tunnel in front of our mouths. In spite of that, the windshield and our facemasks, the cold literally took our breath away if we sped up. Our hands froze despite of our army-special mitts. Our feet, so far, were okay.

Having arrived at our common starting point at the White Alice site, we formed a caravan of the five snowmobiles, two with attached sled for provisions and gas. We headed for the hills behind the site, led by the aforementioned forty-year veteran who supposedly knew the area as you would your own hometown.

I was riding my light little snow machine and Bob was riding his slightly longer and heavier one. While I knew I was not as experienced a rider as the others, and not as strong as the men, it seemed to me that I was having an inordinately difficult time riding smoothly and hugging the icy inclines. I kept getting farther and farther behind the party. Pretty soon I had lost sight of them and getting extremely aggravated that no one, including my husband, was returning to at least inquire about my non-progress.

The weather seemed to be closing in. Soon I was hardly able to distinguish the differences in the terrain, nor could I see the horizon line. My feet and hands were beginning to hurt from the cold and I could feel myself beginning to panic. I gripped the handle bar and throttle to make a last attempt at catching up. I hadn't advanced a hundred yards when a jumble of humanity abruptly loomed in front of me.

Everyone had stopped, and I immediately felt more kindly towards them that they should wait for me. My husband cared, after all.

My humanitarian feelings were misplaced however.

Everyone had stopped because one of the machines had broken down and all were rearranging bodies and provisions on the remaining vehicles.

Bob did inquire as to the reason for my lagging behind. Short temper notwithstanding, I patiently explained that the bumps were killing me and I had to proceed slowly or lose it.

With one of his martyred "Oh...women" looks, he climbed on my machine and gestured that I take his.

The party started up again as we continued our search for the caribou migration path.

My ride was much better on Bob's machine and I was able to keep up with no problem. Because of the fog, I couldn't see how he was doing. In fact, I was no longer able to distinguish anything, including landmarks. I realized that this must be one of those "white outs" that people were always talking about. Pilots caught in one were not able to distinguish up from down and were known to have flown right into the ground.

I concentrated on following the taillights ahead of me, trying to forget about my aching feet and hands. After what seemed like hours, the taillights slowed and then finally stopped.

Our leader looked perplexed and embarrassed.

The whiteout was having its predictable effect and he was just plain lost.

I looked around for Bob, expecting a berating lecture on women drivers. Instead, I saw nothing but frustrating empty whiteness. After a few anxious moments, that did help me forget my aching extremities for a moment, I heard the muffled sound of an engine and recognized my snowmobile emerging from the fog at last.

In sheepish explanation, Bob said that he had figured out the problem with my machine. The shorter wheelbase was the cause. Whereas the longer machines spanned the distance between the regular bumps of the terrain and provided a relatively smooth ride, my shorter machine dipped into the hollows each time, causing a much rougher and slower one. Its lightness didn't help either, causing it to lose traction and control.

Science had absolved the fair sex. I was glad to know that my difficulties were legitimate; not gender-related.

Now that that problem had been explained, the bigger one remained: our being lost. We decided to have some coffee and figure things out.

I took off my mittens in order to take advantage of the warmth of the coffee cup. I felt my face to check for frostbite. Under my chin where my zipper touched my skin, I kept feeling a small lumpy patch of ice. With my fingers, I tried to peel it off to no avail. After a few more attempts, I realized that it wasn't a piece of ice. It was my skin, a solid little patch of skin frozen because of its constant contact with the metal zipper.

To avoid further contact, I pulled my sweater collar over the zipper to protect my throat. It had been an extremely odd sensation to be pulling and scratching at my skin that had no feeling.

Meanwhile, someone decided we should turn around and retrace our tracks in hopes of getting out of the whiteout.

We started the machines only to discover that another one was out of commission. Two people would have to ride in the sleds. In order to make room for them, some of the gas cans and provisions would have to be left behind. We let someone else ride one of our machines and doubled up on the remaining one. We were beginning to leave a trail of belongings that reminded me of "Death Valley Trails" during the Western movement or something. At some point in the future, someone was going to have to come back to retrieve the items left behind.

I knew I wasn't volunteering for that job.

By now, the aching in my feet had stopped and they had simply turned numb. I knew I was having circulation problems that my crouched position was not helping. I also wondered about my new condition: being pregnant. I was pretty sure that the cold wouldn't affect me, but the bumps might. I gritted my teeth against the cold and the jarring ride, hoping that the weather would lift or that our leader would find something familiar to steer by.

Soon we knew that at least we were going in the right direction because we passed our first abandoned snowmobile. After another coffee break and another broken down machine, we continued by instinct and were finally rewarded with the welcome sight of the dishes of the White Alice station.

There was a collective sigh of relief.

We could hardly get off our machines. Hands stiff and frozen, feet like boulders on the ends of our legs, we fell into a truck that someone had generously provided for us to take us home.

All I remember of the truck ride home is excruciating pain in my feet. I spent the entire evening sitting on the floor-heating vent, shivering uncontrollably. Not knowing that I should be grateful for the pain, I felt sure that I would never regain full use of my feet. Later, I discovered that it's when they don't hurt that you should be worried. At that point, it was purely academic. I didn't know how I'd manage it, but I never wanted to see another snowmobile again.

* * *

Bob, however, forgot the pain quickly. Because we hadn't reached our goal of finding the path taken by the migrating caribou herd, he was quick to undertake another venture in that territory and, this time, he did find traces of the caribou migration. Having hurried home, he immediately put together a hunting party by convincing a few victims that it was a "sure thing" hunt. But, they'd have to hurry because the herd was not about to stick around for people to find it.

The hunting party was gone for the better part of a day. At nightfall, my hunter came to get me to show me his prizes.

Having no choice in the matter, I listened to a wild tale of the hunt.

Rounding a hill and finding himself almost in the middle of a huge caribou herd, Bob started firing away. By the time the rest of the hunting party had caught up with him, only carcasses remained, scattered all over the hillside.

Bob stood smiling broadly amid the carnage.

Since he had had to convince them to participate, and since they hadn't been able to fire a shot, the rest of the hunters weren't too pleased with having missed all the fun. There was a lot of disgruntled murmuring as the carcasses were tied down to take home.

Naively unaware of his sudden loss in popularity, Bob gleefully led me over to the school gymnasium presently under construction. I'm sure the architect would have been more than astonished at the purpose his building was serving at the time.

Hanging from the exposed joists in the ceiling, a dozen caribou carcasses twisted and turned in the drafty night air. The whole place was reminiscent of the meat locker in the movie "Rocky."

My heart sank as I realized that our work was cut out for us. Each carcass was about the size of a large calf and would easily provide enough meat for many months. We'd share Bob's take of six of them with our friends. All they had to do was provide the labor to reduce this bonanza to neatly wrapped freezer-fodder.

Reluctantly, I faced the butchering process. Armed with several skinning knives, we began our task. The fact that the carcasses were suspended helped us to perform the laborious skinning process. Inch by inch we cut through the fascia and pulled, separating the hide from the muscle. In the poor light we could see something rather disturbing: many peculiar gooey larva-like parasites burrowed between the skin and the muscle tissue. Vaguely reminiscent of tiny oysters, they were the most unappetizing creatures we had ever come across.

We sent a sample to the University in Fairbanks to be analyzed. There was absolutely no way I was going to cook and eat something that had those things attached to it, at least without knowing what they were.

The analysis revealed that they were harmless larvae, especially in view of the fact that they were not embedded in the meat itself. All the same, as I later unwrapped the neat freezer packages, I could never avoid the recollection of seeing them with the hide peeled back in the skinning process. During the period of time when I was likely to be the most susceptible to morning sickness, Bob insisted on frying his beloved little caribou "breakfast steaks" in the morning. The odor wafted nauseatingly throughout the trailer, and that is the time I came closest to losing my breakfast before I had even eaten it.

Stuff you need for hunting...

✑ CHAPTER 7 ✑

GOVERNMENT IN SPITE OF THE PEOPLE

Firmly ensconced in our cardboard-insulated mobile home, we had settled into a routine that made the out-of-the-ordinary become expected.

Up in the morning in the total darkness. Check the walls of the bedroom for temperature reading: ice patches about six inches above the floor and about four or five inches square. Must be about thirty-five below outside.

Crack open the faucets to wait for the water to flow while having breakfast. The heat tapes worked most of the time to keep the water pipes from freezing, but sometimes they needed a little help. After about a half-hour, the cold water would flow but, for some illogical reason, the hot water line would take longer.

Off to school, quite often with no coat in thirty

below weather because the school building was only a few yards away, I always had a fleeting picture of my parents showing their disapproval when I didn't dress properly.

Back home for lunch at noon and then back at school for the afternoon session.

Each school day brought with it new frustrations partly because the kids were often lethargic and poorly motivated. They saw no relevance in the material presented to them. School was a place to stay warm, and, for the older kids, to sleep off whatever ailed them.

During our first year, with the exception of my successful drama production, we felt as though we were pushing the proverbial rock uphill.

The high school student body was largely made up of native kids from the town itself but there were also some kids from "outside" such as the Episcopalian minister's children, children belonging to the FAA compound, the hospital compound, and native children boarding here from outlying villages. Depending on the year, there were also teachers' children.

This diversity was sometimes an asset but could also be the cause for friction. I always felt particular sympathy for the principal's children, but that's a universal situation. Principal's kids anywhere face particular opposition in any school.

Most of the teenagers lived in a very confined world, had limited general knowledge, and were uncomfortable with their identity. The "native power" movement was making itself felt but they weren't sure of its implications. As we saw it, the people over forty were secure. They were proud of their heritage but were able to look at changes without feeling threatened. They treated everyone with respect and kindness and valued doing their best.

The younger generation however, was at what I call "cultural loose ends." Many felt that doing things the "old way" was uncool and rejected anything to do with it except to pay it lip service. When someone decided to institute an Athapascan language course, most of the students wouldn't have much to do with it.

Some of the older people wanted to keep the old crafts alive and tried to get some interest going in sewing skins and beading. The kids would much rather order out of the catalogs. It was sad to see the culture disappearing with nothing to replace it.

The worst damage to the native psyche however, was done by a group of sentimentalist, mostly white so-called intellectuals, who did more harm than good with their misplaced "do-gooder" attitudes of instituting "native pride." Instead of expending their energies to equip the younger generation with coping skills to ease them into the working world, they simply spouted ways for the natives to reject rules, demand rights, and circumvent responsibilities.

Natives were told that game laws shouldn't apply to them, that taxation wasn't legal, and that they should scream discrimination whenever something didn't go their way. They were told that the government owed them this and that, and that they shouldn't be held to task for anything. This type of brainwashing effectively stripped them of any motivation to approach life in a positive, self-confident way.

This attitude trickled down to the classroom. The teachers operated in that realm of "authority" being much maligned. The students quickly drew this parallel, so our leadership was at risk of being thoroughly undermined.

It reached a point one day, when a petition, signed by a large number of villagers, reached the school, asking that all the teachers be removed. Various reasons were given, not the least of which claimed that we were all biased against the people and educating them to fail.

After some research by the administration, the petition was discovered to be the brainchild of an employee of the University of Alaska stationed in the village to train local college-age native students to become teachers themselves.

The irony was not lost on us.

For whatever reason, he persuaded his students, who had been observing our classes as part of their training, to circulate the petition among the villagers and get them to sign it. In fact, most of the signers had no idea of what they were signing. This was made very evident when one of the elders came to the school and asked to address the teachers as a group. It must have taken an inordinate amount of fortitude for him to fight his culturally ingrained shyness in order to address a group of people who thought they were under fire.

His address was plain, simple, and to the point. He was sorry about the petition and wanted us to know that most of the people who had signed didn't understand what it was. He spoke for the villagers when he expressed his appreciation for what we were doing and felt betrayed by the person who had instigated the entire movement. With awe-inspiring dignity and poise, he asked that we forgive his misled people.

We were only too happy to comply and spare him further embarrassment.

As a footnote, the really guilty party in this was himself eventually removed from the village, but resurfaced in our lives years later, in a different place.

As time moved on, we felt the malaise endemic to the native population. The men of the village missed the validation that a survival economy of the old days had given them. Providing for the family had been a full-time occupation. Everything had had to be done by hand and kept you busy for a long time. The advent of the boat motor, the rifle, the power saw, and the mail-order business, meant lots of idle time and, consequently, boredom and lack of responsibility.

So killing time became a pursuit in itself. Often, this led to trouble.

The women held most of the rare jobs of any importance: post master, mayor, storekeeper, hospital employee, and teacher's aide. In addition, they kept the families together and did most of the domestic chores. The men had been thrown into the time- saving world of mechanical appliances that made their jobs easier, but they hadn't made the intellectual step of modernizing their attitudes. They still didn't do "women's work" but expected the women to maintain the workload they always had. Instead of figuring out a way to turn their extra time into valuable activity, they drank, argued, fought, and sometimes beat their wives and children. The latter often had to go to someone else's house to get some sleep before school the next day.

This reminded us, ironically, of city living at its worst. But here, there was the added danger of being left by the side of the road at the mercy of the extreme elements. Luckily, members of families tended to look after each other. Even the smallest child carried a special awareness about those things. Making sure Mom or Dad wasn't passed out in the cold was a constant concern. One drunken soul actually survived a night out in sub-zero weather because he had had the good fortune to fall backwards into a pile of newly shoveled snow. The only parts of him to be frostbitten were his knees as they were the only things sticking out of the snow.

In spite of the knowledge that any night might find someone involved in a drunken brawl, we never felt endangered going "downtown." People usually kept family concerns private, and we never felt that our safety was in jeopardy even though we went to town dances and social gatherings.

Our first such outing was the New Year's Eve celebration involving all night music, dancing and general partying. Actually in a dress for the occasion, I found myself riding a snowmobile at thirty or forty below, a light coat thrown around my shoulders. I remember wondering if my stockings would hold up after enduring several such trips. My high heels would dig in the snow and keep me from slipping as we went from house to house to celebrate. As the evening wore down, behavior did deteriorate. When arguments became too heated, it was time to hone your avoidance skills or your splitting-up-fight-skills. We absorbed a great deal of insight into the interpersonal relationships of this special world.

"Outside," adult parties meant just that. Children were never given much opportunity to observe their parents in that social setting. Here, to the contrary, children were active participants, often trying to break up fights between relatives or trying to drag Mom or Dad home before they became too inebriated to make it. The ugly scenes they often witnessed actually gave them uncommon skills in handling explosive situations.

There was a certain honesty involved because nothing was hidden. If someone was known to be an ugly drunk, it was accepted as part of this person's character and there were no pretenses about it. If someone's mother liked to sleep around, it was a foregone conclusion that she would probably have to suffer consequences. And most of the consequences for any kind of behavior that offended someone were usually physical.

On Sunday mornings, there was often a full waiting room at the hospital. The Public Health doctors detested pulling weekend duty because it meant calls through the entire night. Because health care was free thereby relieving the patients from any responsibility, they would think nothing of requiring a doctor at any time of night or day. Whether it was for a sore throat, a hangnail, or major stab wounds, the doctor's life was never his own.

One Thanksgiving Day, as we were enjoying our meal at the hospital compound with the two doctors and their families, a call came in from the hospital. The one on duty went over to take care of a stab wound.

Throughout the evening, he was called back three more times, all for the same patient who couldn't quite resolve his hostilities and kept getting into more fights. The doctor finally committed him to one of the beds just to keep out of further trouble.

In the city, an evening of emergency care such as this would have cost thousands of dollars. Here, it cost not one cent, except to the taxpayer.

Paying for any kind of medical care was an impossible concept for most Alaskan natives. The Department of Public Health was probably the most important agency in the state. It provided care of every description at every level. If care in the villages was inadequate, a patient would be flown to the cities by charter airplane, given free board, treatment and medicine. Dental and vision care were included.

I remember one incredulous native lady in Togiak who couldn't get over the fact that I would pay a dentist to "hurt me." Equally inconceivable were the expenses of having a baby.

While this comprehensive free health care extended the life expectancy of the population as a whole, it carried with it some negative implications. One of the constant aggravations for the care providers was the carelessness with which the villagers handled medication. If it took a while before the medication worked, it would be tossed out as "no good." If, on the other hand, it made the symptoms disappear, it would also be tossed out before the ten days necessary for cure. The attitude that there was always more where that came from hampered proper medical procedures. In dire situations, a patient had to be boarded at the hospital just to make sure that medication was properly administered. More than once, we retrieved medicine from the trashcans at school and tried to explain to the "prescribee" the necessity of taking it according to directions.

Alcohol consumption, damaging enough on its own, interfered with medication as well, further hampering cures. Altogether, diagnosing illnesses was the least of the doctors' tasks. They had to change an entire attitude about medicine as a whole. In a way, both our professions worked in concert to educate on this subject.

In its zeal however, the almighty PHS, sometimes overstepped the bounds of reason. Towards the end of our year in Togiak, a PHS agent had become aware that an old man was "suffering" the onslaught of glaucoma. He did have glaucoma, but he had adapted well to his ailment and had a great family back up system so his actual suffering was only a term. In spite of his vehement protests, as well as his family members', the Public Health authorities decided to fly him to Anchorage to perform surgery. Before leaving, he admonished, "I'll die out there." Dismissing this cry for help as the simple hysteria of an old man, the government took him away from everything he knew and loved, and plopped him into the sterility of the big city hospital. We never saw him again and never found out if he had ever been able to return.

We later found out that this approach was not unique. Many villagers had been taken from their villages never to return alive. Many times it was not due to the illness in question. The operations had always been successful. Unfortunately, the patients had died of psychological shock due to intense loneliness and disorientation. Some do-gooders just never left well enough alone.

In Tanana, the hospital played an important role in our lives, much more than in its conventional aspect. It provided us with a wealth of friends. We became close with the doctors and their families, the nurses, and the administrators. In the first years, three doctors arrived at the same time we did. They were putting in time here as part of their military duty. Just out of medical school, they were ready for anything, and were never disappointed. We enjoyed their company because their "talking shop" kept us from spending our whole time immersed in the frustrations of our own profession. It was good seeing different perspectives and gaining new knowledge.

At one point, we instituted our own "Book Club." As a group, we would assign ourselves a book to read that we normally wouldn't choose for recreational reading. It had to be something educational or controversial. Once a month, everyone would gather for dinner or dessert at the house of one of the members and discuss the book. Neither rain, nor sleet, nor sixty below weather could keep us from our appointed book club rounds. It became almost a religion. At any rate, it beat an evening of mindless T.V. watching that would have been the order of the evening in the outside world.

◌ CHAPTER 8 ◌

TRAPPED ON THE TRAP LINE

When not reading, making bread, riding snowmobiles or doing schoolwork, there was always the old hunting and fishing routine. When Bob's winter trap line did not yield much besides a frozen rabbit or two, he decided to extend it.

Trap lines were jealously guarded by each trapper. Grandfather rights were deeply revered; so were uncle Charlie's, and cousin Willy's, and so on.

It was difficult to find an area not previously claimed, especially within reasonable distance of the village. No one would divulge the best areas for trapping, so Bob had to proceed as scientifically as he could: by guesswork.

He decided on an area by a certain creek about thirty-six miles from town. Piling his trapping paraphernalia (a varied selection of traps and snares) on the sled he pulled behind his snowmobile, he set out for the long drive through treacherous winter terrain much as a commuter sets out for work on the freeway.

Among the biggest dangers was the ever-present possibility of slipping into an overflow while trying to cross the many creeks that lay in his path. Ice on a frozen creek or river is not an immoveable object. The layers are, in fact, almost elastic, yielding to pressure exerted on them by accumulation of literally tons of snow. As the ice cover grows heavy and sinks, water is forced up along the banks causing layers of ice, snow, and water to form, resembling a frosty layer cake.

It takes an observant eye to notice the slightly different color of the slushy, water-laden snow that provides warning of the inherent danger of overflow. Bob was careful to avoid the questionable areas and managed to lay his trap line, using fish as bait, without any unforeseen dunkings.

After long hours of exhausting and debilitating work, he returned, greatly satisfied with his day's labor.

Several days later, he decided to go check the line as there had been a heavy snowfall and he was afraid the line might be obscured. One of the hospital employees asked to accompany him, which gave me a small amount of peace of mind.

The temperature had stabilized at about thirty-five below, a relatively comfortable temperature for normal winter travel. Bob's snowmobile pulled his sled with survival gear, as was his habit. As his partner had been around longer, Bob let him lead, confident that experience made a better leader, but worried enough to voice his warnings about the many overflows on the way. They were within two miles of the beginning of the trap line loop when Bob was just about to take the lead as he knew where it started. His partner chose that moment to speed around a curve in the path and slide right into one of the danger spots Bob had been careful to avoid.

The snowmobile slid into five feet of slush and water, its rear end completely submerged, its skis protruding, and its driver immersed to his waist. While he thrashed around in panic, Bob quickly unfastened his sled, positioned his snowmobile on a low part of the solid bank, and forced one of the overhanging branches down to his companion who was now thoroughly suffering.

Pushing and pulling, they were able to extricate him from the water. Once on the bank, Bob helped him roll in the snow in order to create a kind of icy blotter for the water. As the water froze on the snowsuit, it could be brushed off.

They removed the snowsuit and used the same procedure for the clothing underneath. Bob quickly made a fire but there was still so much water in the clothing that thawing it out seemed to make it worse. They used some rope to pull the sunken snowmobile as far up out of the water as they could but it was so coated with frozen slush that retrieving it proved completely impossible. So Bob wrapped the victim, now shaking uncontrollably and emitting huge clouds of steam, in his survival sleeping bag, in the sled. He stuffed small spruce branches around him and tucked a canvas around the whole package in order to insulate him from the wind chill that the ride home would cause.

Then began a very miserable three-hour ride home. Every once in a while, Bob would stop to make sure his partner could move his arms and legs and keep circulation going. A few times he made him get up and walk around for good measure.

Meanwhile, back on the home front, two frantic wives noted the ever darkening and threatening sky, and the lateness of the hour. My stomach and mind were in their usual state of turmoil. I wore out the rug between the living room and kitchen and couldn't concentrate on anything but sponging off the counter and rearranging the cupboards for the twentieth time.

At ten thirty, I finally received a call from the other frantic wife that the trappers had returned. It took another hour for my stomach to untie itself. Then resentment against the cause of my distress rose to the surface. By the time Bob opened the door, and although I was immensely relieved to see him, his welcome was probably two degrees warmer than the creek water.

As he didn't want me to worry too much, he minimized the events of the day. That way, I wouldn't be too worried to let him go on another expedition next weekend.... he thought.

ᕲ CHAPTER 9 ᕘ

HERMIT HAIRCUT

He would come into town on his dog sled, clad in his cold weather gear, looking for a dose of human companionship and entertainment.

One year he came in for an unexpected haircut.

For the better part of the year, Bushy Charley lived in the minds of the citizens of Tanana. On occasion however, he did enter the realm of reality. The story was that he had originally come from California disenchanted with his life, and decided to become the original "bush man" living off the land, dependent on no one.

He had built himself a small cabin, trained a team of dogs and obtained everything he needed from his own "back yard."

No one really knew his age or even his name, and he was the butt of much good-natured derision. His most remarkable physical feature, an incredible mass of tightly matted hair usually crammed into a knit cap, was the focal point of the attention of the gaggle of children who pursued him around town as he did his errands.

His financial status, if he even had one, was negligible, so he had to resort to the cheapest means possible to provide himself with some spirits to celebrate his visit to civilization. Because he could not obtain the elixir of preference, vanilla essence (the storeowners reserved a supply for honest cooks), he resorted to buying cans of hairspray. A good squirt into the cap could send you into blissful inebriation. After an entire can, nothing could wake you for hours on end.

Charley was in just such a stupor when his little retinue decided to alleviate him of the weight of his crowning glory. Carefully removing his woolen cap, the perpetrators snipped away at the conglomeration of curls that had probably not seen a hair-care product for months. The result was less than impressive, especially since the self-appointed barbers couldn't reach the area under his head without disturbing the victim.

Rumor had it that when Charley realized what had happened to him, he unleashed a terrorizing exhibition of anger that deterred any future pranksters from ever considering a similar incident.

In spite of the picture of errant and shiftless behavior he created for the newcomer, he nevertheless commanded respect in his element, the wilderness. It was known that he was such a good tracker and hunter that he had managed to sneak up on a wolf and stone him to death. He'd had several encounters with grizzlies and black bear, and had emerged the victor.

During the coldest winter months on one of his hunting expeditions he suffered a broken leg. Splinting the leg, he managed to get home by dragging himself behind his dogsled. In order to keep a fire going in his cabin, to survive, he had to drag himself from his door across the frozen ground to reach bushes and undergrowth for firewood. For weeks he repeated the process until he had cleared out a large ever-increasing area around his cabin. Eventually his leg had healed enough to get his dog team together, and ride to town for belated medical attention.

And that incident was only one of many of its kind. He had another opportunity to practice medicine on himself when he tried to settle a fight among his dog team. One of his dogs, intentionally or otherwise, bit him in the face and tore his mouth and cheek into shreds. He patched his lips as well as he could with pine needles and headed for Tanana's hospital, a trip that took him several days.

As they did their best to fix the wounds, the doctors were amazed at the efficiency of his patch job and the fortitude he had exhibited performing what must have been an excruciating task.

༄ CHAPTER 10 ༄

BUSH BABY

After our move into the trailer, a JCPenney Trailer Sales Special whose insulation, we discovered, did have an inch of fiber glass in addition to the cardboard previously mentioned, we had to think about making room for the arrival of the third member of our family.

We decided to change our grocery storage room into a nursery. The two extra bedrooms were each about nine by ten feet, not exactly master suites. We figured we had until July to change things around.

Meanwhile, we kept busy at school, and Bob continued to give his snowmobile a workout whenever he had the chance. I spent many a late evening, pacing the floor wondering what dangerous predicament he'd gotten himself into. He'd finally show up, bursting through the front door in a cloud of powdered frost, looking like the abominable snowman. His earlobes were constantly peeling from frostbite, and he had two spots high on his cheeks from squinting that were perpetually red and peeling as well. I don't think our living room was ever free of boots, sweaters, long underwear, mitts and scarves making a trail to the bedroom. There was way too much stuff to fit in the diminutive closets. I gave up trying to put anything away. When the baby came, we'd have to figure out a way to keep things under control. Meanwhile, there were a few other things we wanted to accomplish.

We had decided to work on master's degree, which meant returning to the University of Fairbanks to work on our courses. By June, I was getting pretty large, and fitting in the desks was a snug proposition. In some cases I would forget to suck in my gut, and would get up, lifting the whole thing with me.

This occurrence, however, was not as embarrassing as what had happened when we were registering for our classes.

A professor from the previous summer had caught sight of Bob in the registration line, and, recognizing him, had boomed out for the benefit of the hundred or so bored people waiting, "Well, what have you guys been up to all year out in the bushes?"

At the same moment he caught sight of me and my belly, and answered his own question just as loudly,

"Never mind. It's plain to see what you've been up to."

This effectively livened up the registration process, as I mentally crossed him off my Christmas mailing list.

209

Classes dragged for me, especially since I had to make several trips to the bathroom per class. The weather had turned hot and humid.

I had obtained a doctor in Fairbanks in case I wasn't able to make it back to Tanana in time for the birth. I don't know whether it was genuine concern for my safety or for his potential bill, but he was absolutely opposed to my giving birth "out there in the primitive conditions of the Alaskan bush. They don't even have blood there, if something should go wrong."

I guess he was right, but I had made up my mind that the baby would be born in the village. I had every confidence in the doctors and facilities.

The supposed due date was mid-July, but the fifteenth came and went with not so much as a twitch. By the twenty-fifth, we decided to go back to Tanana for the weekend and see what the doctors thought. We did, and they thought that I was overdue. They decided to take an X-ray to see if there was calcification of the baby's bones, indicating too much time in utero. If I had been thinking clearly or with modern knowledge, I would never have allowed the procedure. As it was, I dumbly submitted.

The X-ray readings were inconclusive so it was decided to "pit" me; inject me with Pitocin. I spent a horrible afternoon being "pitted," ie.: hooked up to an I.V. that was supposed to induce labor if you were anywhere near term.

After several painful hours, it became obvious that I wasn't, because nothing developed. We flew back to Fairbanks and back to class.

We had invited my mother to stay with us in Fairbanks and to be with us for the birth. She spent long boring days waiting for a grandchild who was taking "Indian time" too literally.

Finally, the summer session was over. We did our yearly grocery shopping, and headed back out to the village. My mother was due to leave on the fifteenth of August on a non-changeable flight back to Europe, where she lived.

On the night of the fourteenth, in desperation, a nurse friend of ours concocted a special drink for me made of nine parts castor oil and one part Tang orange powder, the drink of the space-age. I drank it down after having had a huge meal of fresh salmon, potatoes, corn, and blueberry cake. The drink was supposedly a foolproof birth inducer.

At around three in the morning it certainly induced a clearing of my intestines. At five, I felt something other than my digestive system acting up. I told Bob I was going over to the hospital.

Conditioned by weeks of delays, he certainly wasn't your run-of-the-mill panicked father. He groggily acknowledged my plan and waved me on in direction of the hospital, only a few hundred yards away.

At seven, the doctor decided that time had finally come and that Bob was going to miss the show if he didn't get over to the hospital.

I say show, because there was standing room only in the delivery room thanks to all the participants in the event. Several of our friends on the staff, who were not on duty, wanted to assist. A couple of friends and two medical students asked if they could observe as well. There was hardly enough room for anyone to do anything but everybody carried on in a festive mood as I struggled to maintain my composure.

At eight, Bob was still absent, so someone went over to the trailer and banged on the door.

He made it just in time to see his son born and to cut the cord. My mother was able to go home with a photo of her first grandchild barely thirty minutes old.

* * *

Naming your child can be a problem for anyone, but for teachers who've had any number of personalities associated with a variety of names in their classes, it poses a problem of particular difficulty. You want to choose a name that doesn't remind you of some vibrant little character you had to put up with for several long months. We thought about "Castor" humorously in honor of the cocktail that had brought him into the world in time for his grandmother to catch her flight home, but then settled on Geoffrey, spelled the original way. Neither of us had ever had one in class.

We had the next two weeks to get used to having a baby around before school started. I found a babysitter and tried to get a feeding schedule going that would mesh with the school schedule. I would be able to go to the babysitter's house for the lunch break at noon and be back again at three. Most of the time I'd be missing, the baby would be sleeping, so it was a good arrangement. Luckily, he was a good sleeper, making it through the night by six weeks. I did feel fatigue in the early afternoon, and had to fight off an overwhelming desire to doze in class.

ॐ CHAPTER 11 ॐ

BAPTISM BY MOOSE BLOOD

The next milestone was the baptism. We had to catch the itinerant priest when he was in town. There was a resident Episcopalian minister, but the Catholic priest was a pilot of some fame who spent as much time in the air as at the pulpit.

Because he gave the impression of having his feet firmly planted in the abstract world of theology, people were never certain of how he successfully piloted his single engine 'plane, having to deal with such down-to-earth aspects of flying as filling gas tanks and flipping appropriate switches. More than a few times the various control towers lost contact with him after cryptic communications. Ten minutes of total silence followed during which the worst was feared. Then he'd crackle back to life, casually assuring the tower that everything was fine. It was a common belief that he had a special support system up there.

We did manage to nail him down to make an appointment for the baptism. It was to be late the next

Sunday afternoon.

This coincided with the first weekend of moose hunting season. Bob was planning on making the first foray of the year with the doctor who had delivered me of Geoffrey a few weeks before. Promising to be back in good time for the ceremony, Bob left with his usual mix of eager smile and determined frown.

I had my doubts but I couldn't fight the rituals of hunting season. Besides, our freezer was pretty low on meat, as, in anticipation of a successful hunt, we had optimistically forgone ordering any.

I helped gather all the gear together and into the boat.

Early Sunday morning, they cast off and aimed up the river towards Fish Creek, ironically a spot known for good hunting. I waved good-bye, Bob's assurances of being back in time for the baptism ringing in my skeptical ears.

At four that afternoon, I felt the same stomach upset that I always did waiting for my husband to return from whatever venture was at hand. Many a dark cold evening found me in quiet panic, not being able to sit still, eat or sleep.

This time, embarrassment figured greatly in the scenario since I had a priest, a proxy godparent, and a few witnesses all sitting in pews, tapping their feet impatiently, peering down the aisle of the gloomy church.

I kept chiding myself for allowing this to happen. My husband's priorities had always been a little off-center and I didn't know why I had expected the baptism of his first-born to be one of them. At least the baby was fast asleep, not caring that his mother's blood pressure had risen twenty points. The priest cleared his throat, looked at his watch and made a few inquiring noises. I made some excuse about going out to look down the street.

I rushed to the door, glad to get away. I knew the good father was scheduled to say mass in another village that day, and that he was getting impatient to fly his winged steed down river. I strained my eyes toward the point where I knew they would tie up the boat, but saw nothing but a raven picking at something by the water's edge.

According to legend, this bird could be someone's ancestor, and I wondered if he or she was gifted with some supernatural understanding of my situation. Whether he or she appreciated my predicament, I'll never know, as the inscrutable yellow eye blinked balefully at me, wary of my presence. I could see how Poe had imagined a raven mysteriously knocking at his chamber door.

Swallowing my pride, I returned to the dark church and searched my brain for something to say. The baby chose that moment to wake up and get fussy. A little time was spent trying to quiet him and the priest announced that we'd have to proceed right now or wait until he was back in town at some other time. Knowing that the hunting season would not be over for two weeks, I knew it would be an exercise in futility to reschedule.

I was deliberating what to do when the church

door burst wide open letting in a bright shaft of light worthy of the best baroque landscape. Silhouetted against it, superhero style, Bob-the-Hunter stood as if expecting applause.

Actually, having come in from the outdoor brightness, he was momentarily blind, and trying desperately to see if anyone was there in the gloom.

Secretly thanking the gods of kept appointments, and acting as if things were totally normal, I turned to the priest to ask him to begin.

I was surprised to see an odd expression work its way over his features: a mixture of incredulity and indignation. His slight stutter turned into downright stammering as he asked if Bob was going to stay "l-l-like that" for the ceremony. I didn't realize what he meant until I had a good look at the father of the baby, now that he had approached. His camouflage hunting clothes were covered with mud, water weeds, little branches, and most of all, great blotches of blood that didn't stop at the edge of his clothes but stained almost every patch of skin. I was almost as taken aback as the priest.

"Well, what are we waiting for?"

Looking very puzzled by the collective consternation around him, Bob was all business. He scooped up his fussing son, stuck one of his grimy, bloody fingers into the baby's mouth to quiet him, and looked up expectantly at the silent ogling group as if we were crazy.

The stunned silence was broken only by the contented slurping of the tiny guest of honor.

Deciding against apoplexy, the master of ceremonies cleared his head with a shake, opened his missal, and hesitantly intoned the beginning verses of the ceremony. I'm sure that he felt he'd better do an extra thorough job for a child who was obviously going to need all the blessings he could get.

* * *

I had to give Bob credit, albeit grudgingly. He had done what was necessary to feed his family and had made it to the church on time to boot.

After the baptism, during which the moose-blood-covered finger had kept things running smoothly, we rushed back home to outfit me for the "harvesting of meat." I got dressed for the occasion in my best flannel shirts and hiking boots. It was only September, but the evening could get nippy and many hours of previous experience stood me in good stead.

While I dressed, Bob gave me a quick account of how the hunt had gone.

He and his hunting partner had started up the creek, stopping at every place they knew led to an inland lake. Several treks to each of these lakes yielded nothing but tracks.

Eventually they reached the spot that had the reputation of giving up a moose every year. They knew that no moose had yet been brought back to the village this season, and were hoping to get this year's prize.

After fighting their way through the brush, they

came to a large opening and immediately saw the long lake extending a quarter of a mile away from them. At the very opposite end, they could barely make out something at the far edge of the lake.

"There it is."

His partner began to crash through the undergrowth until Bob grabbed his shirt to stop him. He whispered hoarsely,

"Hey. We'll get him from here or you're going to scare him back into the woods."
Bob tapped his ex-elephant .375 rifle.

"This'll knock him down."

The other hunter looked at him skeptically and whispered back.

"We're way too far. That must be three hundred or more yards. Even if we wound him, he'll make it back to the woods and disappear."

Bob gave him a smile loaded with smug superiority. In his best back woods vernacular he reassured his partner: "He ain't goin' nowheres when he gets hit with this baby." He lifted the rifle and lined the moose up in his crosshairs. His partner did the same. Two deafening reports tore at the afternoon air. The chirping and woodsy noises were immediately replaced by a few seconds of dead silence. They blinked towards the far end of the lake.

"Oh my God. Where'd he go?

Bob grimaced in the afternoon sun, trying to locate the curiously absent prey. At loss for an answer, his composure almost slipped, but then he caught sight of something slowly rising and just breaking the surface of the water.

It was the tip of an antler. The moose had fallen without being able to make even the smallest move towards the protection of the trees.

The .375 had eminently illustrated the "he dropped in his tracks" cliché. Unfortunately, as the great white hunters were soon to discover, he had been making tracks in a very deep section of the lake. Even if the shot had only wounded him and he had just been knocked down, the poor animal probably would have drowned in the slimy depths. As it was, the undeterred hunters waded out as far as they could, used a branch to pull the carcass towards them and then set to the task of gutting it to avoid any contamination of the meat while they returned home to make the church appointment. As the submarine characteristic of this venture had been an unlikely contingency to say the least, snorkeling apparatus was not part of their equipment.

The surgical implications of the operation were not lost on the medical man as he enthusiastically wielded his overgrown scalpel. Gutting a moose was an arduous task under the best of circumstances. Trying to accomplish the same on a half-submerged animal that bobbed up and down and sideways seemed a hopeless one. Our two hunter/butchers attacked the problem with naïve energy. After opening the belly, they managed to pull everything out that could cause the meat to spoil. They propped open the stomach cavity with stick in order for it to air out and dragged the twelve-hundred-pound animal to the shallowest spot possible where it would have to wait until they returned.

As time moved relentlessly on, and Bob harbored the image of an irate wife waiting for him to show up for his son's baptism, he prodded his partner into fast-forward mode. The trip home was of record speed and, as previously illustrated, there was certainly no time for a change into church-going clothes.

* * *

We dropped off our bundle of joy with the other hunter's wife, gathered one of our nurse friends, and hopped into the boat. We had had no time to pack food or drink but figured on only a few hours work for the job waiting for us.

We had strapped a canoe onto the boat because retrieving the meat was going to be a three-stage affair. From the river, the canoe would be carried to the inland lake where the men would paddle it to the moose carcass on the far side. They would load the meat and ferry it from the far side of the lake back to a spot on the near shore where our friend and I were waiting. Then the four of us would carry the chunks of meat through the brush about a quarter of a mile to the waiting boat down on the river.

Anyway, that was the plan.

Light was quickly disappearing as we drew up to the unloading spot. We tied a Coleman lantern to one of the paddles and rigged it on to the front of the canoe.

We all helped carry it through the woods and to the edge of the lake. The men climbed aboard to find their prize, leaving us by the water's edge in the gathering darkness.

Thus began one of the longest nights of my life. The ground was too wet to sit on so we had to stand for hours while the surgeon and his assistant made manageable pieces out of the largest deer in the encyclopedia. Sound carried over the water and we could hear an exasperated Bob telling his doctor friend to quit naming the various muscles and get on with the butchering.

In spite of my layers of clothing, I realized I hadn't worn enough because the damp was chilling me to the marrow. We tried to ward off the cold by walking around in circles, but didn't want to stray too far from our appointed spot. We told each other our life stories twice over.

Still, no meat on our side of the lake.

After several hours, we saw the light approaching. The canoe contained a daunting mound of bloody meat. Bob put a forequarter on my shoulders and I almost crumpled under the weight, especially since my frozen fingers couldn't get a good grip on the meat and it kept sliding off.

My memory of the next few hours fails me. I suppose it happens to people when they engage in activities that cause them mental harm. I do remember telling myself that we were set for the year as far as meat was concerned and that every screaming muscle was saving us hundreds of dollars. All I know is that we made dozens of trips from the lake, across the field, through the woods and down a slippery bank to the riverboat into which we dropped hundreds of pounds of meat. Even the heart and liver weighed an extraordinary amount.

The ride home I spent in a stupor, but was quickly shocked to reality when, as we barely stepped through our front door, the school bell rang for first period to begin.

We were much too exhausted to stamp out much ignorance that day.

"Nevermore..."

❧ CHAPTER 12 ❦

FILLING THE PANTRY

There was no rest for the weary after the school day was over, either. We had left our year's supply of meat in the boat and now we had to carry it up the bank and store it, before we could carve it, package and label it.

During the end of the summer between our son's late arrival and the first day of school, a few of the hospital staff joined us to build "Ye Olde Moose House."

It consisted of a square structure that looked like an oversized, totally screened-in gazebo. We hung all our moose sections from large hooks in the ceiling. The screen let in the breezes and kept out the flies etc. Several days of hanging would tenderize the meat and give us some slack time to organize our freezer wrapping system.

We (hunters and wives) settled on a date for the

butchering and decided to use our kitchen as the butcher shop. Centering our kitchen table in the middle of the floor for easy access, and covering it with a sheet of plywood to serve as gigantic butcher block, we set up an assembly line of carvers, sorters, wrappers and labelers.

In order to ward off the thirst that would necessarily accompany this strenuous work, someone had provided a mysteriously obtained case of beer.

One of the men fetched a hindquarter from the "moose house" and plopped it on the plywood. It was immediately set upon by eager butchers brandishing saws and knives of every size and description. The meat was then cut into meal-sized pieces, passed to the sorter who organized it by type, ie.: steak, roast, ribs, or meat for grinding. It was then passed to the wrapper with the appropriately sized freezer paper. This person double wrapped it to protect it against freezer burn and passed it to the labeler who dated it and provided a description of the enclosed cut.

At first this person had no trouble determining what name to use because the butchers had been careful with their cutting. After a while however, many packages received the label "miscellaneous roast" and "stew meat" because, as the butchers attended more and more to their thirst and less and less to their business, the meat cuts began to defy any accurate description. The really ragged pieces were added to an ever-mounting pile that would be ground into moose burger and moose sausage.

Some cuts were a puzzle to deal with. The ribs were so large that they had to be sawed in half or in thirds to fit in a normal oven. The neck was difficult and ended mostly in the ground meat pile, which would be a whole other evening's entertainment.

By the end of the session, we had three piles of wrapped meat, one for each family involved, and a smaller one for our nurse friend who had helped load the meat into the boat. We also had a very messy kitchen and a huge mound of meat for the grinder.

At three o'clock in the morning, I was cleaning the last scraps off the linoleum and Bob was putting the last packages in the freezer outside that would be unplugged as soon as the weather turned permanently cold. The beer bottles would be dealt with later.

We went to bed with a comfortable feeling of knowing that we had a freezer full of provisions. There's something about returning to the most basic form of survival—something about being self-sufficient that immerses you in the warmth and comfort of satisfaction.

For many years thereafter, whether it was having canned fish, put up berries, frozen vegetables from our garden, or stored any kind of food that had not been obtained the conventional way, we invariably experienced the same satisfaction and we always slept very well on those nights.

front quarter
moose

* * *

For the next few years, this hunting season ritual was repeated with variations. The hunting partners changed because the hospital staff changed every two years. As Bob gained experience, his new partners would receive their initiation into the local idiosyncrasies of the hunting process.

It was common knowledge that moose taken at the height of mating season known as "the rut" would taste very strong due to the hormones raging in his system. A desperate or inexperienced person could "call one up" by rubbing an old antler on dry grass or trees. Any moose answering the call would be heavily in rut, looking for a fight. One of the new doctors brought home such a

227

moose, proudly displaying a record size set of horns. His pride was soon replaced by embarrassment however, when people would joke about the smell pervading the entire hospital compound coming from his kitchen at dinnertime. No one would ever accept a dinner invitation either...

Some years we would send our frozen to-be-ground-moose meat to a company in Anchorage that would combine the meat with suet and make moose-burger or sausages.

Other times, we would do it ourselves.

One year, one of our associates possessed a sausage-making machine. What a boon that turned out to be. The process would probably not have been as comical as it turned out to be were it not for the beer that flowed freely throughout the evening, but the silliness grew to gigantic proportions, literally. Since it's up to the person filling the sausage skins to determine the size of the sausage, he has to be reasonably alert to pinch off the ends for each link. The sausages kept increasing in length in concert with much joking and gutter variety humor. Some were fat, some were skinny and no two resembled each other. It was good thing the product was for private consumption. We made potato sausage, Italian, Polish and many combinations thereof.

During the year, as I would unwrap a package of oddly shaped sausages for supper, I'd have to chuckle as images of inebriated sausage-stuffers came to mind.

⤸ CHAPTER 13 ⤷

RUNS WITH WOLVES

One hunt did not result in any meat wrapping. It was one of those things that just happen and you have to seize the moment or forever regret it.

Anyway, I guess that's how Bob looked at it one day, as he was cruising the countryside in his snowmobile in the eternal quest for likely prey. The latter was supposed to be the ever-elusive caribou but as he scanned the countryside from the top of a sharp ridge, a small movement about a half-mile away caught his attention. At first he thought it was a lone caribou, separated from the herd, but realized immediately that the size and gait were wrong.

He signaled to his riding companion and both took out their binoculars. They could hardly contain their excitement as a wolf came into focus, trotting easily on the frozen snow, in no apparent hurry. That a wolf pelt could bring in several hundred dollars was a minor consideration as both throttles opened up to maximum speed.

The speedometers read upwards of fifty miles an hour as the chase led the prey and the pursuers across frozen hill and valley. The wolf seemed able to maintain his speed indefinitely, and Bob was awed at its ability to maintain its footing on the glaciated surfaces of the steep inclines. He was gaining on the animal when it reached a rise and seemed to founder as it disappeared over the knifelike ridge top. Too late Bob realized the cause, as he sailed over the ridge top only to find there really wasn't another side. Airborne, he looked down at an incredibly steep incline that fell away as he and his machine reached the end of the arc created by their trajectory. Realizing that he was better off landing away from his machine, Bob pushed himself away from it and braced himself for a jarring encounter with the earth. He slid and rolled, and finally came to a stop, halfway down the sheer hillside.

The machine however, didn't come to a stop until it had bounced first from end to end, and then rolled sideways, parts flying off, gas cap included, so that the gas was spurting out of the tank. When it finally rested, it was minus its windshield, part of its cowling, the rifle, the scabbard, and the sled.

Supplies littered the hillside. Even the drive belt had snapped off.

Never put off by small details, and determined to

catch up with his quarry, Bob hurriedly righted the machine, replaced the belt, tore off a piece of hanging cowling, and hoped there was enough gas left to continue the chase. His partner, meanwhile, having led a more conservative chase, was just rounding a corner, intact.

Still in sight, the wolf slowed as he tried to traverse a virtually glass-like surface that didn't seem to provide the least foothold.

Having hastily restarted his machine, Bob was gratified to find that it was still operational. He opened the throttle and tried to hug the hillside, as did the wolf.

Leaning far to one side, he tried to balance himself, but the machine kept sliding.

He was close enough to the wolf with its ear hanging, and scars showing, to see it clawing and scratching to stay on the side of the mountain. Then the animal finally reached a spot where he was able to get a more effective grip. Glancing quickly back with what Bob could've sworn was a sneer, he broke away from his pursuer, who was struggling mightily just to stay upright.

As he slid down the mountainside, slowly at first and then with ever increasing speed, all Bob could do was look disappointedly at the wolf's claw marks left on the ice where he had scratched himself to safety.

A few moments later, as both panting hunters sat on their machines, contemplating what had just happened, and they squinted at the small silhouette of the triumphant wolf, inching its way toward the horizon, they had to admit ruefully that the score was entirely uneven.

In the other direction lay the remnants of a survival kit, hunting equipment, machinery, and lunch, including small pathetic packets of cocoa powder strewn over several hundred yards of glaciated terrain.

⮞ CHAPTER 14 ⮜

MIDNIGHT SUN FRUIT

One summer we decided to get together with some of our hospital friends who stayed in town for the summer to plant a vegetable garden.

Summer was our favorite time of the year, and although it meant fighting off the July mosquito (also known as the Alaska State Bird) and the August "no-see-ems" (an almost invisible irritating insect that bit ankles and wrists unmercifully), it also meant long lazy days in the perpetual sunlight, berry picking, picnics, potlucks and a casual attitude about everything.

Berries of all types were particularly plentiful in the neighboring undergrowth, and I learned to make a variety of cakes and pies to use them to their best advantage. The only problem resided in the ever-present danger of competing for the berries with the bears who enjoyed them as a staple in their diet, and who were only just a bit less fearsome than the mosquitoes.

We never went berry picking without a trusty .44 in the bucket along with the berries. The mosquitoes however, proved to be much more of a menace than the bears.

By the time the children grew old enough to play outside all day, I used to spray them once in the morning and once in the afternoon with repellant, and send them on their way to the playground. I realize now, with new science, that it probably was not the best thing for them, but it certainly seemed like a good solution at the time.

As the weather didn't turn warm enough until the end of May, in order to give the garden a head start, we grew "starts" in containers inside the trailer house. At the beginning of June we sectioned off a plot of land with a wire fence, tilled the ground, and then planted our seedlings. We'd all take turns weeding and watering.

Because of the long hours of daylight, the vegetables not only grew quickly, but incredibly large. To this day, when I see zucchini squash in the supermarket, I flash back to the ones we grew thanks to the midnight sun. As I stuff a dozen little green things in the plastic bag, I recall that just one of those from our arctic garden was too much for a family of four. They grew to two feet long and five or six inches in diameter. In addition, we grew huge cabbages and several types of squash. Our greenhouse provided a great place for tomatoes, pickles and cucumbers.

By September, there was an incredible harvest for a garden of its size and, all three participating families had a freezer full of fresh frozen vegetables. Thanks to the garden, that year, we only had to make a very small food order at the market.

It was that year also that, with our "garden" partners, and fighting off the July mosquitoes, we built our own sauna out of logs. We made a cursory plan for it and began to lay out the logs just as kids used to do with Lincoln Logs. We notched the ends, laid fiberglass insulation between them and lifted, pushed and pulled until we had a reached a decent height for the roof.

We built a partition dividing the sauna into two small rooms: one for changing clothes, and one for heating. The plywood roof came next and then it was time to install the fifty-gallon drum stove. Over the top of the stove, we placed rocks encased in chicken wire to increase the heating surface.

By the time the construction was finished, the first snows had fallen and it was ready to be tested.

After several winters, I think my sweat glands had atrophied because I could never get a good sweat going like everyone else seemed to be able to. I just turned extremely red and uncomfortable, and had to get out after only a short while, leaving the other occupants to enjoy themselves. Eventually, I figured out a system whereby I would exercise a little bit first, and get my system going.

The sauna ended up being the only way I was ever really warm enough throughout the winter.

"You must be related to Sam McGee," Bob used to say as I commented that I had finally found a place where I was really warm. "Maybe you'd feel even better if you sat inside the stove, right on the live coals like he did."

So be it. Robert Service would've understood. It beat sitting on top of the heating vent in the trailer, waiting for the fan to blow lukewarm air up the back of my shirt.

*　*　*

It was time for Geoffrey, now with a full year of Alaskan living under his little belt, to have a sibling.

We had a kind of "race to pregnancy" with one of the hospital couples who wanted a baby too. At almost the exact same time as two years earlier, we knew we could expect another little bundle to carry around in my parka. We beat the other couple by a month or so and knew that the mothers-to-be would probably not be going on next year's hunting expeditions.

As the winter progressed, it got harder and harder to load Geoffrey onto my back inside my parka, and still zip us both up. I was now carrying around thirty or so extra pounds both in front and in back, but it was still easier that way than having to bundle the kid up every time I wanted to step outside.

Riding behind Bob on the snow machine was harder because it was getting to be a tight fit and I was getting hampered in my attempts to encircle his waist with my arms. Pretty soon I had to switch parkas with him to accommodate the growth of both babies. This worked fine until warmer weather made the parka unnecessary.

🕭 CHAPTER 15 🕭

ALMOST HOME ON THE RANGE

During the last year, we had spent some time thinking about investments. Enjoying the highest teaching salaries in the nation didn't do much good if they weren't put to some use. We had missed out on many ventures because we had been so reluctant to part with our savings. We might have risked life and limb many times, but the old bank account was sacred.

I'm not sure how the seed was planted, but Bob got wind of an outlandish idea. Instead of settling for a duplex, an apartment complex, or a normal piece of land to buy for investment purposes, he found us an entire island. It was called Sitkalidak, and it was located just south of Kodiak Island, hundreds of miles from us. He had many conversations with a real estate agent from Anchorage, and made a long trip to see the property. It was actually a cattle-ranch whose cattle had gone wild

237

and were providing the local Kodiak bears with plenty of meals. There was a young couple stationed there as caretakers for the various outbuildings, the bunkhouse and the main residence.

The whole place brought out every molecule of romanticism in Bob's body. It embodied everything he had ever dreamed of by satisfying his affinity for "The West" (every book ever written by Louis Lamour graced our book shelves), "THE WATER" (we have every magazine from Boating to Yachting), "THE SKY" (ditto for Airplane to Western Flier) and "THE LAST FRONTIER" (nickname for Alaska). Absolutely nothing could shake this morsel of life from his firmly clenched jaws, including my profound dislike for the real estate agent involved in the deal.

Against my ever-wary instincts, we signed the necessary papers, turned over a great deal of money, and planned our summer trip there. That I would be eight and nine months pregnant (due in July) without a sure way of getting to the mainland only made us stop to think for a minute.

Oh well, we knew how to have a baby and our doctor friends gave us some "birth out of attendance" forms. I had not had any complications and Bob has always had this impression that I could handle any physical challenge. The minute was quickly over and thoughts dismissed.

We planned to pick up my mother in Anchorage on the way as she flew in from Europe again.

Case closed.

It was an impressive place, but to say that it did not have all the comforts of home would be to minimize the situation. We couldn't stay in the main house because of the caretakers, so we had to take the bedrooms in the bunkhouse. The water heater didn't take its job seriously, the oven and stove needed extraordinary means in order to cook anything and the whole place had a grimy, unkempt feeling about it. Washing clothes was an all day proposition because the ancient washer had to be operated partially manually, and partially through prayer.

We ate meat from the scattered herd and knew immediately that we'd never make money from that source. The cattle had been feeding on the scrub brush and grass, and were probably in the best shape of any of their bovine relatives in the rest of the world. They had no fat on them and ranged so far and wide, up hill and down that they exercised more than a full time aerobics instructor and were just as stringy. I tried marinating, pounding, breading, boiling, baking and grilling the meat to no avail. It was always a challenge to the jaw muscles. We longed for a good, tender moose roast. The only respite we had were occasional king crab from the crab pots.

We sucked those shells dry.

Our days were pretty boring. We had no television, no phone and very little company. Once or twice we rode the tractor and three-wheelers across the island to the beaches on the other side. That side of the island was a duplicate of what I pictured Hawaii to be:

white sandy beaches, deep blue ocean, and frothy surf surrounded by rocky cliffs. The sand dunes were a local addition. The only discrepancy was about thirty degrees of temperature. We would have spent more time on that side had it not been for my reoccurring fear of bears. It wasn't just that Kodiak bears are the largest and meanest in the world, but there was no way we could have gotten away from them if they had decided that we were intruders. The tractor moved at about five miles per hour and we had no weapons.

There's something about being pregnant, having an almost-two-year-old, and your mother with you, that makes you feel skittish in the face of the unknown, especially when your husband is off reconnoitering somewhere else. So, on our slow trips back and forth, I kept an eye on the cattle scattered about the hillsides, knowing that a panicked cow would be a warning sign that something was wrong. I was hoping the bears preferred beef to humans. But, the closest we ever got to bears the entire time as far as we knew, were some tracks in the mud, and I think they had been there a while.

The only visitors we had in the six weeks of our experimental stay were the real estate agent for a couple of nights and our pregnant friends from home. My due date had come and gone as in a bad case of déjà vu, yet it was certainly a blessing. We couldn't even have boiled water too well, had the need arisen.

The radio, our only form of communication with the mainland, worked about as well as everything else. I didn't really have much in the way of baby stuff. I guess that even before we had left home, I had the definite feeling that the baby was going to be as late as its brother had been, and I really never thought I'd give birth anywhere but at home. I should have been a prophet. Our doctor friend was very disappointed that he couldn't perform the delivery in these primitively romantic circumstances, but I really could not have said I'd be glad to oblige him.

The six weeks were up and it was time to make the four flights back home, but not before our usual date with the grocery store that we kept in Fairbanks as I dragged my belly up and down the aisles.

This time my mother went home before the happy event, not wanting to put off her return flight. I guess the island experience made her scramble back to the comforts of her home.

By the 14th of August, the day before Geoff's scheduled birthday party, I began to think that my children would never be on time for anything, if their births were any indication. But Geoff was destined to have a baby sister instead of a party, because in the evening of the fourteenth, I was being delivered of her, and his party had to be cancelled.

Most of the day, I had spent the time between contractions doing a kind of last minute cleaning. School was starting in two weeks and I had to straighten out everything so we'd have extra room for the new baby. When the contractions came too close together to separate, I finally walked over to the hospital so that the staff would have time to get ready. Bob dropped

Geoffrey off at a friend's, and joined the party in the delivery room. At about seven thirty, Natalie Anne announced her arrival with a yell, and then promptly fell asleep.

I hadn't wanted any anesthetic or painkillers of any kind. If I had known better, I would have at least allowed some for the sewing up of the episiotomy. As it was, the experience of being sewn up without any painkiller was worse than the birth itself. I don't know what I had been thinking. The doctor made a special note that the procedure was by my request so that if anyone ever read the records, they wouldn't blame him for being sadistic.

Had Natalie been born on the east coast instead of the west, they'd have had the same birthday. In fact, however, after taking an extra few weeks, she had rushed into the world beating midnight by a few hours. At least, this time the father had been there in plenty of time instead of napping through the preliminaries.

I couldn't spend more than a day in the hospital because, besides rescheduling a postponed birthday party, I had to help put up some more vegetables from the garden that had been tended by our friends, put away the year's groceries, freeze a bunch of fish for the winter, get the children's room organized, get the baby on a feeding schedule, and, oh yes, the job; I had to prepare for school.

And school meant more time this year because of the completed gymnasium: basketball teams. We had spent the previous year introducing it during physical education classes and this year our school had been included in the regional basketball schedule. In addition, cheerleading was introduced. All of this meant that our school day was to be lengthened and our weekends abbreviated. Because we had a babysitter only during regular school hours, I had to take the children to all after-school activities. Geoff knew quite bit about basketball by the time he was three, and enjoyed going to all the games.

It was amusing to see the development of the students who hadn't held a basketball before. They were deadly serious about their games and there wasn't an empty spot on the bleachers whenever we held a home game.

The Tanana Wolves were making their mark.

☙ CHAPTER 16 ❧

THE GREAT AIRPLANE VENTURE

With two children to take care of, I became more housebound and settled into a routine. There were no more spur of the moment excursions by snowmobile or boat for me. Bob, on the other hand, decided to widen his transportation methods.

Enter the airplane era.

It's difficult to avoid the issue of planes in this state, when almost all significant transportation is through this means. One of the new doctors had a Cessna that he used routinely to get groceries in Fairbanks.

One particular routine that developed because of this was the Ritual of the Feast of Saturday-Morning Doughnuts. The doctor would fly to Fairbanks, buy several huge boxes of fresh doughnuts and summon the entire hospital compound, plus us, to someone's dining room. We'd brew several pots of coffee, let the kids play together, and have an orgy of doughnut eating. People who have been able to buy them at any time cannot understand why such a big deal can be made out of something as ordinary as a doughnut.

Some things just have to be experienced to be understood.

I guess the doughnut episode served to drive home to us what owning an airplane could mean in terms of being able to get things whenever we wanted them. We had gone so many years doing without the things that other people take for granted every day, that the unforeseen availability of something was almost like getting a Christmas present. Having our own plane would open a whole new world. We could have fresh milk, vegetables, parts for the vehicles etc. whenever we wanted or needed. We could even travel to other places, including weekends on the town in Fairbanks.

Through forgotten circumstances, Bob discovered that the plane belonging to the itinerant priest was for sale. The two-seater Citabria seemed the perfect starter for a novice.

One day soon thereafter found us and a few friends, wheeling the future "doughnut getter" through the compound, right up to our bedroom window. There we planned to tear off the old and faded paint to replace it with a brand new coat. This project threatened to occupy our entire summer because we certainly could not rely on experience to speed our progress along.

In order to allay the fears of anyone who might be

horrified that a total ignoramus can put together a machine on which lives could depend, it must be

From her spot on a hospital gurney, Natalie (1 yr.) supervises the process.

understood that the Federal Aviation Agency requires that there be periodic inspections at each stage of the work. If a mistake is made, it is rectified on the spot.

Actually, I was surprised at the stark simplicity of the structural aspect. A few wooden pieces, some no thicker than a finger, a few aluminum braces, and some canvas was all that separated a body from the earth when the whole thing took off. A bicycle seemed more complicated if not more structurally sound.

The project did take the better part of the summer. I was responsible for the crowning touch: painting on the large call letters that identified the airplane: N8318V—"One-Eight-Victor" for short.

I carefully made a template to the specifications required and laboriously traced the outline to be filled in with bright red paint. The machine was now ready and needed only a pilot to fulfill its purpose.

The pilot however, was only in the making. Because there were no instructors immediately available, Bob and one of our hospital friends who had also just purchased a plane, hired one who would fly in periodically from Fairbanks.

In the meantime, Bob put in every spare hour he had, madly taxiing up and down the runway at our little airport. He was probably the only one ever to put in more ground time than airtime in the history of flight.

There was method in his madness however. This constant taxiing gave him such familiarity with his machine that he was able to solo in record time; after only a few hours of instruction, when the instructor finally did arrive. We cut off his shirttail, as is the custom, to celebrate the first solo.

A new era had arrived. In addition to the ice, cold, wildlife, and water, I could add the sky to the elements threatening my husband's life.

And threaten it, it did, usually in the form of the weather.

We thought we needed a new variety of groceries one day, and Bob decided to mix a cross-country exercise with some shopping.

"one-eight Victor" 18V

The weather forecast was not particularly noteworthy that day, so he set off in the direction of the nearest supermarket: the Safeway on Airport Road in Fairbanks, over a hundred and thirty air miles away.

That seems like more than the usual trip to the corner grocery store, but when you gotta have some fresh strawberry pie and real whipped cream, you'll do pretty much anything to get it.

Anyway, it was a good excuse to use the toy.

The student pilot plotted his course (a straight line to the east) to Fairbanks International, and jumped in his plane.

The trip went without a hitch. Bob just knew he was getting the hang of it.

The grocery shopping went without incident too,

except that the shopper got a little too enthusiastic about the groceries and overestimated the room in the plane. He had to crowd many items around himself, and hoped they didn't get in the way of his piloting efforts.

As he took off from Fairbanks, he noticed that visibility had lessened considerably, but there was still enough for an easy flight straight west. After all, he had received the okay from the tower. So what if they didn't know it was his first venture that far from home.

Making his way, he noticed a definite increase in the darkening of the sky. He was asking himself about the turbulence that might lie ahead. Not being able to see behind him, he was not aware that there was much more to be feared from back there. This was a case where ignorance was, if not bliss, certainly a little peace of mind.

"I should go around this," thought the pilot. "Or should I go under it? How about over it?"

These were all reasonable questions. While he was contemplating what to do, his ride became bumpier and bumpier. The windshield was suddenly streaming raindrops. Lightning flashed and thunder exploded around him.

Gathering the sum total of his few weeks' experience, Bob decided to ride it out, figuring that that if there was massively bad weather around, he would have heard about it at the airport.

This was just a little squall. It couldn't last.

Suddenly the plane began a series of leaps and bounds, dislodging some of the tightly packed groceries.

Batting away boxes of cookies and rolls of toilet paper, Bob tried to get a grip.

Visibility was getting less and less. He couldn't see the horizon. In fact, he couldn't see much of anything.

Another flash of lightning.

Although it made him jump out of his skin, the brightness enabled him to see that he was just over what he recognized as Minto Flats.

That meant he was still on course.

Thanking God for the favor, he tried to fly using what landmarks were slightly and occasionally visible. It worked for a few minutes. He tried to relax his shoulders and neck tightly bunched with tension.

But the ground was rising at an ominous rate.

The damned hills!

He had forgotten about the rise in elevation between Minto and Tanana.

Well, he couldn't very well feel his way around them in the darkness.

There was only one thing left to do. He'd have to go slightly off course to the south and follow the Yukon. The tree line was much heavier along the river and would afford him a stronger mark to follow.

Banking to the south in the gathering gloom, he could just barely pick out the tree line and the snaking river.

Decreasing altitude, he skimmed the trees, hugging them as though they were a lifeline...which they were.

Flying over the Yukon, desperately trying to keep

it in sight by playing touch-and-go with the treetops, he had no time to give thought to the fact that we had once just as desperately negotiated the river with a frying-pan-oar.

That desperation paled in comparison.

As Bob painfully made his way westward, he eventually saw the confluence point of the Yukon and the Tanana.

Home!

He realized that his jaw ached from clenching his teeth, and that his hand seemed to have a permanent iron grip on the stick. He had to peel his fingers back with his other hand to let go of it.

All that for a few measly groceries we didn't even really need.

When we finally got everything home and unpacked, the kids and I could hardly wait to sample our new supplies. Bob was still feeling a little unsettled, but also little proud that he had emerged unscathed by his ordeal.

In fact, the only casualty in the episode was a box of Oreos that had fallen and become crushed between Bob's foot and the rudder pedal.

∂ CHAPTER 17 ∾

FISHING BY REMOTE

As involving as flying was, Bob still had to find something to do during the summer months while he wasn't airborne. He decided to become more involved in the fishing industry.

Since the time of our first sightseeing trip on the waterways around Fairbanks, we had been intrigued with the fish wheel, an invention originating with the Scandinavians who had brought it to Alaska decades ago.

It was an ingenious device that allowed for "absentee fishing" as we called it. Made of sturdy wooden poles, it consisted mainly of two wood and chicken wire baskets rotated by two horizontal paddles pushed by the river's current. The paddles, propelled by the current, forced the baskets to act as a scooping barrier to the salmon running against the current on their yearly quest for headwaters of their birth stream.

The salmon, trapped in the rising baskets, slid down a chute into a storage box. The box was checked twice a day and the salmon harvested.

The fish wheel itself was secured to the shore by more poles usually at an outcropping of the riverbank, just above an eddy where the fish were known to rest before moving back out into the current to continue their ultimate odyssey.

Bob had observed that profits to be made were directly proportional to the size and speed of the rotating baskets, so he decided to build a lightweight metal wheel with oversized baskets. The area around our trailer immediately became a jumble of rebar, chicken wire, and welding material. The kids had to learn to avert their gaze whenever they went outside in order not damage their vision by the light of the welder.

Days of welding mania followed. Slowly the structure took shape and, incredibly, the date of launching approached. This event in itself posed several problems. We decided that the wheel would have to be transported, piecemeal, to a convenient spot on the riverbank, reassembled on the shore, and towed by boat to the fishing site.

We had bought an old open back station wagon that served as transportation for the parts. Bob reassembled all the parts on the gravelly bank, surrounded by a growing pile of tools and materials, constantly reminded by the Yukon lapping at his ankles that time was money.

The salmon run was beginning and he didn't even know if his invention would do what it was supposed to.

Alexander Bell and Christopher Columbus couldn't have proceeded with any more faith. We towed the reassembled contraption to the site we had chosen upriver. We secured it to the shore by stringing poles made from tree trunks together, and fastening them at the shoreline.

We watched with knotted stomachs as the baskets began their rotation. Remarkably, it worked as engineered and gained momentum even as we stared. We were certain the baskets dipped and lifted at least twenty percent faster than the conventional wooden wheels.

Bob made some final adjustments, admired his handiwork for a few more minutes and was rewarded by the sight of our first salmon indignantly flopping against his chicken wire prison as he slid down the chute and disappeared into the locked fish box. The latter, of course, was insurance against marauding "fish box looters" who had the energy to steal but not to build their own wheels.

That evening, the first trip back to the wheel marked the beginning of a six-week routine. Every morning and afternoon found us motoring upriver to collect the contents of the box. We'd dump them carefully into the bottom of the boat until, on a good day, there was hardly enough room to stand.

Then it was back down river to a large sandbar to meet the small 'plane that collected the fish for a cannery miles away.

As long as the wheel turned, so did the profits. It behooved us to make sure that it turned unimpeded. Occasionally, an uprooted tree or log would lodge itself in the wheel causing it to stop until we arrived to clear it.

Ironically, the only thing that interrupted the process for any length of time was the prey itself. As we rounded the bend one morning, just before reaching the wheel, we immediately noticed that it looked alarmingly wrong. The baskets were stationary, and one of the paddles hung limply to one side. The chute was awry, one of its sides loose. For a fleeting moment we feared vandalism. Bob was ready to strangle the culprit.

As soon as we checked the contents of the box however, we were surprised to discover the culprit: a fifty-pound king salmon. Fifty pounds of feisty muscle had dealt the blows that had caused the destruction of its nemesis.

It took us several hours to make the wheel operational again. The salmon, biologically reddened by its programmed phase of development, took up most of the floor space of the boat. The children, whom we had brought along for the ride, sat in the prow, bundled in their life vests, huddled as far from the red beast as they could. The fish was longer and heavier then either of them and they weren't convinced that it wasn't going to get up and attack them.

Sometime later, they weren't at all sad to see it disappear on the "fish plane."

A broken Yukon fish wheel.

Some of the catch Bob was saving to make fish strips with, known to some as "squaw candy." It involved cutting the fish into long one-inch strips, hanging the strips over a wire or twine, and smoking the whole collection for several days. A great deal of oil would drip from the strips in the process, and the meat would end up being dried enough to be preserved throughout the winter.

Often, these strips were the villagers' main food supply, handy to pass out to the children at any time of day if you didn't feel like preparing a meal. Our kids loved them as a chewy snack and it was much better for them than cookies and candy.

Bob's vision for the whole smoking process reached grand proportions. He didn't want just a few bunches of strips. He wanted to make enough to be able to sell hundreds of pounds of them. Thousands of pounds...

Anyway, this venture was going to require a center of operations.

He made the acquaintance of one "Herman the German," an old timer who lived by himself way up the Yukon, but had a fish camp not too far from Tanana that he tended in the summer. We don't even know if his name was really Herman, or if someone just coined the phrase. He had somewhat of a muddy past as an ex-German soldier, and never talked about it.

At any rate, right there on the Yukon riverbank with easy access to the fish supply from the fish wheel, it was the perfect place for building a smokehouse of great proportions.

Together, they came up with a design for the ultimate in smokehouses. Actually, they simply embellished what Herman already had. The result was a many-tiered contraption made of wood and tin roofing. It could accommodate many hundreds of pounds of smoking salmon.

They carefully considered the appropriate heights for the drying racks, the correct setting for the fires to produce optimum quality smoke, and the appropriate time for the process.

Every day, new salmon would be brought in, gutted, sliced, put on racks and smoked. When the first strips were almost done, they'd be moved farther back and replaced by newer strips.

It was painstaking, numbing work, but at the end of a few weeks, there was and impressive collection of fish, hanging, ready for harvest.

Finally the day came when the strips were at their peak of perfection. Tomorrow would be the big day for collecting it all.

We went to bed early to get plenty of sleep before the next day's work.

That night however, someone banged on our door. Blearily, we stood in the doorway in the dusky light of three in the morning, listening as one of the villagers breathlessly informed us that a smokehouse up river was in flames.

We didn't need a crystal ball to know whose it was.

Bob's panic-filled trip upriver confirmed our fears. The smokehouse was, itself, being smoked. Herman was running around trying to throw buckets of water to douse the flames, but to no avail. The fish oil fueled the flames in spite of the water. They watched helplessly as weeks of work went up in smoke.

It was a cliché for sure.

It was lucky that the smokehouse had been in a fairly open spot, or there might have been a forest fire as a result.

During the next week, people had all sorts of reasons for the fire. Not one included accident. Everyone knew it had been set, and many probably knew who had done it. It was up to us to figure out who were the perpetrators and what their motive could be.

We knew that not many people liked Herman. So it could have been hate. We also knew that there was resentment that we had such a large operation by village standards. Some natives did not appreciate strangers adopting their ways. So it could've been jealousy or just plain hostility.

It was a very uncomfortable situation to know that, every day, you might be passing by the person who disliked you enough to ruin weeks of your hard work.

It has left a bad taste ever since.

🦕 CHAPTER 18 🦕

THE PSYCHOLOGY OF DARKNESS

People often ask if the long hours of darkness of an arctic winter affect a person's moods. At the time we were experiencing this phenomenon, we didn't notice any day-to-day differences. We did encounter some rather odd events because of the cold that provided some tense moments at the time, but that make a rather comical picture in retrospect.

After a long day at school, we picked up the two kids from the babysitter's. We crunched our way home over a deep layer of dry, compact snow and opened the back door only to be greeted by geysers of water spewing from the floor heating vents. The trailer floor was covered in an inch of water. In addition to the carpeting, all the supplies we had stacked under the bed were sopping wet.

We put the children in a dry spot and tried to understand what was causing this interesting predicament. When we noticed the full bathtub and the floating diapers and pail, the answer dawned. As usual, we had opened the frozen hot water faucet in the tub in order to get the water flowing. The diaper pail had been sitting on the tub drain. Because of the extreme cold, the pipes did not thaw in time for us to leave for school and we had forgotten to turn the faucet off.

We could only guess at what time the pipes had finally yielded and the water had begun to fill the tub, not being able to drain because of the diaper pail. It must have taken a while but as the tub overflowed, the water had run down the vents into the heating ducts. Every time the heater had cycled and the fan had come on, the forced air caused the water to spew up through the heating vents, thus causing the impromptu fountains that had greeted us as we walked in the door.

Trying to dry out a trailer full of carpet in sub-zero weather poses a daunting task. The school janitors brought over a wet-vacuum cleaner to deal with the carpets. The solution to the water-filled heating ducts was simplicity itself. The janitors simply poked holes in the ducts to let the water flow to the ground.

The fact that from that moment on our heater would be spending double time in its efforts to heat the trailer and the outside because of the precious heat escaping through the same holes the water had, never seemed to be cause for thought. It's possible that the escaping heat actually helped thaw the pipes under the trailer and water would trickle out of the faucets a little sooner than before.

From then on, cold weather or not, I was religious about checking faucets before leaving the house.

*   *   *

Upon looking back, I now realize that the darkness did put most people in a very different frame of mind from that of the summer months. Because we were so busy with raising two small children, trying to make an educational impact at school, tending to our survival activities etc., we never really stopped to evaluate our emotional states.

I remember enjoying the quiet of the classroom during the first few hours of the day when the darkness seemed to envelop everyone in a cocoon of silence. As daylight spread, the kids would emerge from their stupor and the usual push, poke and pull antics would begin.

By the end of February, daylight and darkness were about equal and activity increased. It's true that many people feel depression during winter's darkness and are prone to behave in extreme manners. To illustrate the point, one must first understand the depressing impact cold and darkness can exert on a body. Because the body tries to conserve heat from the inside out in order to protect the important organs, just being cold can inhibit voluntary action. I can remember having to wage battle with myself to take off my mittens to change sparkplugs on the snowmobile to get home. I hardly had the motivation to take my hands out of my pockets to do it. I could have easily just sat there as lethargy got hold of me.

You don't feel like moving even though your life may depend on it.

*   *   *

The following story shows the depressing and horrifying impact that cold and darkness can impose. We learned about it because two of our boarding students, a brother and sister from an outlying village, were summoned home one day.

Their little brother needed them.

A little boy, having spent the night at his friend's house, trudges home in the duskiness and numbing cold of the early morning hours. He's jacketless, expecting in a moment, to feel the gratifying warmth of the stove in his kitchen.

Instead, as he pushes open the front door, he's greeted by more darkness and penetrating cold.

Puzzled, he looks around for the elements of his familiar world. He can tell there hasn't been a fire for hours.

Stumbling in the darkness, and shivering in his thin shirt, he finds the wall switch and flips it on. He gets his bearings in the weak pool of light cast by a single bulb.

"Mom? Dad?"

Greeted by unusual silence, he's drawn to the back room of the house that serves as the only bedroom.

Shaking uncontrollably, he enters the doorway and waits for his eyes to get accustomed to the gloom. Straining, he can see shapes on the bed.

"Mom?"

A few steps and he's by the bed. It takes several seconds for the scene to register.

The dimly lit bodies of his parents are draped grotesquely on the bed, lifeless, in congealed plaques of dark bloodied sheets.

Still shaking, the little boy stares at one hand clasping a knife in the rigidity of frigid death. Another hand has its fingernails totally outlined in frozen blood.

No one knows how long the little boy stands looking at his parents' bed, trembling in the gray cold.

For whatever reason, winter's psychology has claimed two more lives and irreversibly affected several more, including the two children who are called back from their boarding home in Tanana to join their younger brother for their parents' funeral.

* * *

The long hours of winter darkness, the forced togetherness imposed by the hostility of the outdoors, and the idleness endemic to a population that no longer has to spend every waking hour tending to the necessities of life, all contribute to the family confrontations with tragic endings.

In addition to the murder-suicide recalled above,

our six years in Tanana served to illustrate how close to the surface lies the despair and the violence that it sometimes causes. It became obvious to us that some families were more prone to violence than others. Wife beating and fighting were weekly, if not daily, occurrences. Typical of domestic quarrels anywhere, they were never solved with a call to the city trooper. By the time he reached the house to which he had been summoned, no one seemed to want to press charges. The next day, a wife would go to work with fresh bruises and mental scarring, but no resolution to her problem.

Sometimes it would be a parent.

One especially beleaguered family had among its many members four sons who were constantly embattled. One trip down river, ostensibly for fishing purposes, almost became the mother's last. One of her sons, an ex-prisoner for attempted murder of his brother, wanted to push her overboard while another son defended her at knife point. The defender won the battle and each member lived on to continue the war.

One of her youngest, a boy of fifteen, was in one of my classes. In his young life he had already been involved in murderous acts. He had stabbed an uncle, and shot at another family member.

One day, as the kids were writing, he suddenly came up to my desk, slipped behind me, and held a large hunting knife to my throat.

"I'm going to slice your white throat," he said calmly, as he held me in a vice, his blade fractions of an inch from my trachea.

I tried to keep his attention away from one of the other students who was trying to get out the door to go for help.

The incident ended up with the principal and other teachers coming to my rescue.

The next week, the student was back in class; the law didn't address those kinds of incidents.

We never knew the reasons for the discord that seemed to erupt continually among these family members, but we never failed to empathize with the mother who kept the family running despite the continuous turmoil.

It was from this family also that my main play character of years before had come. The youngest son of this family was the young man who had laid aside cultural superstitions and volunteered to lie in the coffin for the sake of the performance.

In spite of his obvious binding biological relationship to the players in his family drama, he was able to look at the conflicts with a more clinical eye, partially because he had experienced life outside the village, and partially because his intelligence had permitted him to gain premature wisdom and understanding about relationships.

Unfortunately, this awareness proved to be a double-edged sword; it had the negative impact of causing him great sadness in seeing the dysfunction of his family.

The day he was himself drawn into the conflict was the day his life took a defeating turn.

For whatever reason, he became embroiled in a fight with his father during which he broke the latter's jaw. His father was flown to Anchorage for extensive surgery to repair the damage.

Apparently ridden with guilt or self-disgust, the son could never reconcile his feelings. From what we could understand, because he was particularly sensitive and basically good-hearted, he could never put this event behind him.

We're not completely certain of his motivation for his following actions and the actual development of events is partially testimony, partially hearsay, but, one evening in late winter, he is supposed to have made a date with his girlfriend to meet at his house. He had told her that if there was no answer when she knocked at his door, she was supposed to push the door and enter. Whether she thought this strange or not, we never knew. We do know that she did follow his directions that evening.

The sight that greeted her, as she grew accustomed to the gloom, would cause even the most jaded soul incredible shock and horror. The young man's tortured mind had finally forced him into the only action he knew would release him from his thoughts. A shotgun blast spattered that mind across his walls and ceiling and left no doubt to the observers that he meant what he had intended.

The above incident, horrible in itself, made a further indelible mark on my memory.

During the great questioning period that usually follows an incident of this sort; when everyone tries to make sense out of the event, and tries to find the reason for such action, it reached me that I was being indirectly blamed for the suicide because I had, years ago, made the young man lie in that notorious coffin for my class play.

Some superstitions are difficult to shake off, and incidents such as these only serve to reinforce them.

According to most documentation, suicide among young Indian males is more common than in any other ethnic group.

Given the small population of the village and the relatively short time we lived there, the two such suicides we indirectly witnessed confirm the statistics.

Besides the one just recounted, there was another one that actually took over a year to come to its final conclusion.

For whatever reason, one of the older teenagers, a poorly motivated student who had begun to appreciate school because of the outlet basketball had provided him, decided one night in the dead of winter to put a shotgun to his throat, under his chin.

He had left a party with a hint of what was on his mind. A friend followed him out and soon realized what was about to take place as the barrel of the shotgun rested at the boy's throat. A tug-of-war with the barrel followed. As the would-be rescuer pulled the tip of the barrel away from the throat to the chin, the trigger was released and the shot missed the lethal mark but erased the young face in a blast of fire.

A half-inch farther out, the load would have missed altogether. The doctors were immediately summoned, and a plane chartered to transport the patient who had to be held in a sitting position so as not to drown in his own blood.

For several months he was kept alive and treated in a Seattle hospital. He was given psychological counseling and was eventually released to the hospital in Tanana. It was thought that although his physical wounds were massive, and no one was sure how much he could actually see, he seemed to be psychologically balanced. The nurses tried hard to distract him and play games with him while testing his abilities. He seemed to be recuperating well, and had no apparent life-threatening condition.

Yet, one day, after having joked with the nurse and having eaten well, he turned on his side toward the wall and died.

The shocked medical staff could only gather that the patient had never wanted to live and that he had, in effect, willed his death even months after his first failed attempt at it.

The nurses who had spent months trying to help him and who had made his rehabilitation a labor of love, spent years trying to accept the tragic conclusion to the life of their young patient.

These events, sobering in any context, seemed more acute in the small world of the village. Added to the accidental, almost yearly drowning of someone from the greater Tanana area, the deaths served as constant reminders of how fragile life can be.

We always felt that the awareness of this encouraged many of the villagers to live totally for the present—indeed, we saw very little preparation made for the future.

Drink could make the unpleasantness of the day go away as well as the consequences of tomorrow. Money was made to be spent—not saved, nor invested. There was an overriding mentality that things would never change..." so why fight it?" In fact, there was a definite resistance to change, most souls finding comfort in things as they had always been.

Off to the races!

Yukon River
Tanana 1976

CHAPTER 19

MUSH!*

Each season brought with it the habits and routines of the year before. The summer meant fishing, the fall meant hunting, the winter meant trapping, and the spring marked the highpoint of dog racing.

Tanana hosted the Yukon River Dog Races to be held in the bright spring days while the river was still frozen solid. It gave everyone the opportunity to shake off the winter doldrums.

---

*From the French Canadian Expression: "En marche!"

By now there were more hours of daylight than darkness and people felt their energy returning.

Years of living with barking dog teams spread out over the village had never really infected us with the sled-dog mania that others succumbed to. We had watched local races from afar and had listened to the progress of the Iditarod race through all the media hype. We liked dogs, but in small numbers.

One of the teachers had lost an eye thanks to a low twig on the dogsled trail. Many dog owners' lives were consumed by harvesting, preparing, cooking and passing out dog food every day of their lives. Mushing could be a romantic's idea of transportation, but we felt that, in spite of their balky nature, snowmobiles were still easier to take care of.

That's not to say that we didn't appreciate the time, energy, and dedication it took to practice this sport.

For the dog races, dog mushers from all over the state and even some other states, showed up to test their teams against the best dogs of the trails. Tanana was known for having bred some of the best dogs in the state.

Different courses were laid out on the river. There were races for every number of dogs to a team; even a one-dog race for the very small children.

I don't know whose idea it was, but somehow we got Geoff and Natalie signed up for that race. There was only one problem. We didn't even have a pet dog, much less the sled type...

What they never got was field experience. Race day would be the first day they would do it for real.

Luckily, one of our fellow teachers had a dependable sled dog he'd be willing to lend us for the event.

We had a look at the beast. He was a sturdy, good-looking Husky, but we weren't convinced of the wisdom of this whole thing. There were definite dangers inherent in riding a fast moving sled on a rock-hard frozen surface. We really didn't know if the kids could hang on for the quarter-mile course.

To the children, this mode of transportation presented nothing new. They had seen more dog sleds than automobiles in their short lives. But they had certainly never driven a sled. At two and four, they were barely as tall as the handle bar. Bundled in their snowsuits, they could hardly spread their legs wide enough to reach both runners.

No matter. They would train for this event.

First they got to know the dog. He was pretty mild mannered for a sled dog, but I never really trusted him. His mouth was even with the kids' faces and his huge canines were always apparent. I'd seen him devour his dinner in a minute flat.

Second, they would stand behind a chair and pretend to drive it, yelling, "Gee! Haw! Whoa! Mush!"

When the day came, it was about twenty degrees and bright sunshine.

Ready for the race? Let's MUSH!

It took a half an hour to get outfitted for the event. The first layer to go on was underwear and cotton socks. Then long underwear and another pair of socks, this time wool. Then a turtleneck sweater. Then some kind of regular long pants. Next came a wool sweater, down vest, and finally a snowsuit. Strung through the snowsuit on "idiot strings" were down-filled mittens with a pair of smaller gloves inside. ("Idiot strings" were the best defense against losing mittens, and the kids wore them for years. I crocheted a set of them for every jacket they ever wore.)

We debated whether to put on regular snow boots or Indian mukluks, finally deciding on the latter because they would be less slippery on the runners. A stocking cap almost completed the outfit. The hood of the snowsuit was held firmly in place by a wool scarf. We tucked the ends of the scarf inside the hood because many people have been strangled or hurt by their own scarves when they get caught in something.

By the time they were fully dressed, the kids looked wider than they were tall. As they moved they reminded us of little robots with stiff arms and legs. The only exposed part of their bodies, noses and cheeks, were pink just with the effort of moving around and of being excited.

Outside, the dry snow made its particular squeaking under our footsteps. It had piled up all winter and was still four or five feet thick where it had originally drifted between the buildings. The drifts were as solid as concrete. Whenever we walked across them, we were reminded of the time that one of the older teachers had had to call school one day because she hadn't left her trailer all week end and, on Monday, she couldn't get out her front door. The snow had drifted so high that the maintenance people had had to dig a tunnel for her to get to school. The tunnel lasted all winter.

Arriving on the riverbank, we looked down on what looked like chaos. Dog teams meandered everywhere. People moved about and some ran as they followed alongside the racecourse, cheering someone on.

We finally found our friend and slid down the bank to set up for the one-dog race. We tried out the sled for size. Geoffrey was able to get a good grip on the hand rail, but Natalie's small two-year-old hands were so stiff because of all the thicknesses of mittens that she had to hang on to the sled by folding her hand all the way over the rail and hanging on by her wrists.

I was worried that she'd fall off, and I was about to tell her that maybe she should wait until next year. Then I got a look at the part of her face that could be seen inside the small tight circle of ruff on her hood. Even scrunched, it radiated determination. I think it would have taken a crow bar to unhook those little mittened hands.

Little did we know that we would see that look for years to come as she later entered competitive sports that gained her a full ride to college.

Race time.

Well, we only had one sled, so they would have to take turns. Luckily, the racers would be timed individually as they each took their turn. The one-dog race was simply a straight line from start to finish. No turn-around to worry about

Geoff went first. He got on the runners, held on to the handle bar and stood proudly as we walked him to the start. Our friend held his dog in check. He lined the sled up in the order required.

Bang! The starter fired.

The sled lurched, but Geoff stayed on as if he'd been racing all his life. He gripped the handlebar as the dog loped off in the direction of the finish line. We ran as fast as we could in the same direction but he was there way before we were. He had a very good finish time, but we couldn't stand around to discuss it, as we had another racer who needed to start.

We grabbed the sled and stood Natalie on the runners. Our friend led her and the dog back to the start to wait for her turn.

She applied her wrist grip again, and I was just sure the start would loosen it. She was absolutely motionless, fully intent on what lay ahead. I was beginning to wonder if she was a normal two-and-a-half-year-old child. Kids older than she were whining, crying and acting up. She just stared straight ahead.

Bang!

Natalie's head snapped back a bit, but she held on. Slightly bent at the knees, she looked as though she was going to lose her grip at any moment. The dog trotted along, ran a little, and then sped up to the finish line.

She had made it.

And then she wouldn't let go. We had to convince her that the race was over, and she could relax her iron grip.

We found out later that Geoff's time had been the second fastest. Unfortunately, they were only awarding first prize. So I made each of them a special certificate that they've kept to this day. They were both exhilarated by their races, and just knew that they wanted to be professional dog-mushers when they grew up.

∂ CHAPTER 20 ∽

ON THE ROAD AGAIN

During the school years, Bob had often been to Fairbanks or Anchorage for in-service or athletic trips. This gave him opportunities to talk to teachers from a variety of towns throughout the state.

We were now expecting a third child and were beginning to think about moving back to the city so that the kids could enjoy some of the opportunities of civilization. At the same time, we were afraid of the negative aspects to city living, even in the far north.

City life has its good points and bad. Life in Alaskan cities is no exception.

Through a chance meeting in a hotel elevator, Bob struck up a conversation with a teacher from the small town of Homer, south of Anchorage. She mentioned that there was a position opening at the junior high school for which Bob was qualified.

From her description of Homer, it seemed an ideal transition between the bush and city living. It was a very small town but it boasted all sorts of favorable characteristics: beautiful scenery, beaches, an artist colony, fishing, tourism, an amateur theater, a good school system, hunting, and access to Anchorage. It sounded like a perfect place to raise a family, especially since it didn't seem to suffer from the diseases of the big city. We were both immediately interested in finding out more about it.

Bob made a short trip to Homer and was guaranteed a job at the junior high school.

We had to decide whether or not to sacrifice two jobs for one. The decision was not made lightly but we had some savings and assumed that, eventually, there would be a job for me.

So we decided to that the time had come to leave the bush and try our luck with civilization. We hoped that our decision would serve our children well and tried to quell our fears of the unknown.

We decided to make a family trip to see if we'd like the new surroundings.

Four airplane rides took us to our prospective home by the sea. We stayed at "Land's End, a rustic hotel at the end of the six mile spit of land that juts out into Kachemak Bay and for which Homer is famous. We walked the beach, saw examples of the local marine wildlife as well as of the local inhabitants. We took in the harbor, the small town itself, and the ever-present gleaming bay reflecting the mountains and glaciers in the background.

We weren't surprised to learn that Homer was known as the " Shangri La of Alaska." The whole picture was almost overwhelming and we knew that this was the place for us to raise the family.

A quick visit to a real estate office resulted in our buying an old Cape Cod type of house in an older residential section of the town. Even though it was located "in the city," it afforded a spectacular view of the bay and glaciers and had a large yard.

No debating was necessary. We signed the papers, took a snapshot of our house and flew back to Tanana to start the packing process.

After selling six years worth of accumulated junk that ranged from a hospital gurney which we used to wheel equipment from place to place, to our freezers which had carried us through many hunting and fishing seasons, we packed our clothes and detached the extra room Bob had added on to the end of the trailer which we had used as an extra family room. We sold it to someone who added it to his house.

We sold our 1947 Ford pickup truck, our fishwheel, and our snowmobiles. The plane had to be stored in Fairbanks. We bought our second Landcruiser from a nurse at the hospital who had it stored in Fairbanks. We had to pick it up on our way south. We said good-bye to our friends, and took one last look around our trailer home to see if we had forgotten anything.

There was a lollipop on the floor. For lack of a better place, Bob stuck in the hole in the ceiling that had supported our "Johnny-Jump-Up."

We learned later that the next tenants interpreted that as a gesture implying that who ever lived there were "suckers." I suppose that the title fit if they expected their home to provide normal comforts and protection from the elements. We wondered if they'd be able to correctly calculate the number of degrees below zero according to the frost buildup on the inside of the bedroom wall.

We had always been able to come to within five degrees or so.

*   *   *

As we left Tanana, we didn't realize that we'd never again use our winter parkas, never fight the vicious July mosquito, the August "no-see-ems," nor the numbing cold of the Alaskan interior. Smoke from the chimneys would forever rise instead of hugging the sides of cabins as it descended to the lowest point it could, and the kids would never hang on to a sled in a dog race on the Yukon ice in the early Arctic spring. We'd never go berry picking with a .44 magnum in the berry bucket in anticipation of bear-meetings (we were wrong on that one), and never check the fish box at our fish wheel. Even the hospital that had witnessed the birth of our children was slated for partial shutdown of services, and the White Alice site was going remote with a ninety-percent reduction in staff.

But perhaps the most devastating development yet to come to Tanana was television. We had heard that its arrival was imminent, but were fortunate not to have to witness the actuality.

We felt that it wasn't just our stay there, but an entire era that had ended. It made leaving that much easier.

PART III

⌘

HOMER AT LAND'S END

⌘ KACHEMAK BAY ⌘

Whipped to a frenzy by the southwest wind, the waves tossed their frothy crests, gathering momentum from each other to crash on the rocky beach. At high tide, their force pushed everything they encountered ahead of them forming a snaky ridge of debris that inched higher and higher up the beach. White clamshells, gray driftwood, pink crab shells, and sections of rotten planks that might once have been part of a boat, all crept inexorably upwards. Long strands of brownish-green seaweed tumbled and curled around everything, knotting them selves together to form a long necklace of sea gifts. Here and there, tumbling chunks of coal shone like black pearls in the snaking necklace.

Below the surface of the sea, at great depths, hardly affected by the tumult above, a three hundred-pound halibut wallowed about, testing clamshells, crabs and other sea-bottom residents for dinner. Hardly anything threatened her, so she didn't need to be particularly watchful for predators even though she was gifted with two eyes on the top of her head to serve that purpose. She hadn't reached this size for lack of food or for fear of other creatures. Unhurried, she continued her search, unaware that summer had arrived. Summer meant July, and July meant "Halibut Derby." While her size made her unlikely prey for the creatures of the sea, the predators she needed to fear were the land creatures greedily interested in her, precisely for her size.

Above, the wind continued to tease the sea and sent gusts through the copse of spruce trees standing guard atop the low cliff. A small clearing afforded a perfect spot for and unobstructed view of the bay. A bald eagle sat on the top branch of one of the swaying trees. Then, in a flash, it flew out over the water, dove talons first into the tops of the crests. Effortlessly and smoothly, it rose into the wind with a struggling salmon firmly clenched in its claws. Aiming for a dry spot on the beach, it lightly touched down. The wind ruffled its feathers as it began to tear into its meal.

And the wind, gathering the momentum of a small gale, signaled the scent of the kill to the ravens, the gulls, and more eagles, who all considered it an open invitation to dinner.

KATHERINE NORBERG

HOMER

Homer Halibut: at 150 pounds, this one will feed the family all year. Summer 1976

Spring visitors in the yard of the beach house.   1978

286

This lump of coal won't be going in a Christmas stocking!

∽ CHAPTER 1 ∾

THE NOT-SO-DEEP SOUTH

We didn't have time for much of a backward glance as we picked up our new jeep in Fairbanks and headed down the road to Anchorage, a trip that would take at least ten to twelve hours. The long hours of sitting in one position made the trip particularly uncomfortable for me at my late stage of pregnancy. I tried to be interested in the spectacular scenery, especially around McKinley Park, one of Alaska's prime tourist attractions, but my seven-month-pregnancy-discomfort prevented me from feeling unbridled enthusiasm. The road provided a driving challenge not only with its unpredictable hairpin turns and steep grades, but with the contortions of the asphalt caused by the extremes in temperature changes throughout the year.

As we neared the outskirts of Anchorage with an empty gas tank, we looked for an open gas station. Because of the daylight, we had lost track of time and didn't realize that the stations closed in late afternoon, daylight or not.

Signs of habitation were few and very far between with absolutely no restaurants or places to stay. After passing three more closed stations, we began to fear the worst. Finally, we found another closed one and decided to wait there until it opened the next morning.

We wrapped the kids in one of the sleeping bags we had brought and put them on the floor of the back of the jeep. They thought it was kind of fun—an unforeseen camp-out.

The story in the front seats was rather different. No matter how I twisted and turned, accommodating the gear shift, I could not get comfortable enough to doze even for a few hours, especially since my bladder constantly reminded me of my condition.

It was another one of those long nights indelibly imprinted in memory. All I could think of was getting to Anchorage and taking a long hot bath at the hotel.

The owners of the gas station were in no hurry to open the next day, probably figuring that there wouldn't be any customers for a while.

As they unlocked for business early next morning, they were very surprised to find four disheveled human beings at their pump.

Tired, sore, and very hungry, but now with a full gas tank, we completed the last few dozen miles into the center of Anchorage. I took my long-awaited bath and felt human enough to face the next challenge of the day: picking up my mother at the airport and then four and a half more hours of driving, the last leg of our journey to Homer.

This time we could appreciate the scenery because we knew the trip would be shorter and we were beginning to feel some excitement at reaching our destination.

Leaving the mountains behind, we made our way down the Kenai Peninsula noting the devastation left behind by a forest fire a few years ago. Acres and acres of blackened hulls of spruce trees lined the highway giving the entire area a strange, almost alien atmosphere.

We passed the outskirts of Kenai and then Soldotna, closest towns to Homer. We never envisioned the hundreds of trips we'd make to those two towns in the subsequent years.

We went by some more villages, including an old Russian settlement, Ninilchik, and then caught sight of the Pacific Ocean gleaming a hundred feet below the road. Across the water stood Mt. Redoubt, an active volcano, one of several in a network to the west.

The view, enhanced by clear weather, provided a satisfying exhilaration that stayed with us until we rounded the last curve at the top of the hill before Homer.

We were not prepared for the extraordinary sight that greeted us at that point. From a height of a several hundred-foot precipice, we could see a hundred miles in every direction except north, from where we had just driven.

An arm of sheer mountains lined the south, reflected in cobalt water, providing a backdrop of glistening, snow-covered mountainsides and glaciers, uninterrupted at the waterline since their reflection was as true as they were.

The bay itself set off the small islands and peninsulas as velvet might set off a jewel collection. There was enough moisture in the air that small pockets of clouds hugged some of the hillsides in contrasting softness to the rocky cliffs.

I had never seen such a richness of blues, grays and greens in one spot.

To the east, we could see Homer itself and the spit extending into the bay as if trying to reach the mountains on the other side.

As many times as we rounded that last curve to Homer in the years thereafter, there was always anticipation of that truly breathtaking panorama. Since the weather and the light were so changeable, the view was almost always different, and always provided an emotional lift.

It was difficult to tear ourselves away from the vantage point of the cliff, but we were soon wending our way down the steep road, integrating ourselves into the scenery. This marked the first time in seven years that we were actually able to drive to our home. It felt like a small luxury.

We had less than a month in which to make the house livable before the baby arrived.

The house was pretty old and there were some major inconveniences in its structure. There was no bathroom upstairs by the bedrooms, the foundation was a foot larger than the house itself, so rain would leak into the basement, and the back porch was so piled with junk that we couldn't open the back door.

On the plus side, it was only minutes from the stores and the neighborhood was quiet and safe for the children to play in.

We could never get enough of the view either.

The summer temperature was cooler than we were used to after six summers in the hot and muggy interior, but there were fewer bugs, and a total absence of forest fire smoke that had often plagued us up north.

Altogether, we were very satisfied with our move.

☙ CHAPTER 2 ❧

THE WAFFLE STOMPER

Stephanie Lynne arrived a week before her siblings' birthdays, thereby keeping all our birthdays, except Bob's, in August.

Because we were now subject to normal hospital care and the bills that go along with it, Bob made me hold out past midnight in order not to have to pay an extra night's stay. Lucky for him, I was too preoccupied to argue.

Once we got to the hospital, we actually had a few minutes to spare before Stephanie was born.

I spent the next day there, trying in vain to catch up on sleep. The kids came to see their new little sister and were awed.

The very next day, I found myself getting groceries at the market, juggling my less-than-two-day-old baby with a grocery bag.

Meanwhile, as Bob was getting ready to go back up to Fairbanks to finish getting his pilot's license and logging some flying time in his plane.

It was taking a while to get our telephone hooked up, and when Bob left a few days later, we still didn't have a functioning one.   I don't know why this fact bothered me, because our neighbors were close and nothing seemed very threatening in our new environment. I guess there's something about a mother protecting her brood that makes her particularly sensitive to these things, or maybe I had a premonition of something happening.   Whatever the cause, I was edgy after Bob left, even though my mother was still there to help out.

My edginess proved warranted the very next day.

It started when I was just about to take what I was counting on to be a long, hot, relaxing bath. Covered by a towel, I was about to immerse myself into soothing water when, for some unexplained reason, I had the impulse to walk to the window. As I pulled back the curtain, an arm flashed by the pane as though someone had leaped backwards to avoid my seeing him.

I knew the window was much higher off the ground than a person's height and that whoever it was had to be hanging on to the window ledge in order to be able to see in. So, whoever it was, wasn't there by accident.

Still holding the towel to cover myself, I burst out of the bathroom, yelled at my mother to grab the kids and herd them into the living room. I dove under the junk in the hallway that covered Bob's .44 pistol, slipped off the safety, and the lights.

Pistol brandished, I warily approached the doors to lock them. There was a sudden noise on the back porch that I knew was piled with old furniture and belongings left by the previous tenants. No one would be able to sneak around there without causing a major commotion.

Slowly turning the knob, I then threw open the door, pointing the pistol barrel out into the darkness in my best imitation of Elliot Ness.

I heard one thud and then complete silence.

Towel flapping in the draft, and realizing what a preposterous and very unlike-a-federal-agent-picture I must be presenting, I came to my senses, yelling at my mother to put coats on the kids while I dressed myself.

We piled into our jeep and sped downtown to the police station. I don't know what they thought as the five of us crowded through the doorway of the diminutive Homer Police Department, but they kept straight faces as I explained what had frightened me.

A car was dispatched to follow us home so that the officers could inspect the premises.

On the outside wall under the bathroom window, the officer's flashlight revealed muddy scrape marks. There were wet footprints on the porch in front of each living room window. The police preceded us, guns drawn, into the house where they made a methodical inspection of each room and the attic. They did the same in the basement.

Apparently, the intruder had not entered the house.

"Well, I guess you guys just had a visit by the 'Waffle Stomper' tonight," revealed one of the officers.

Totally mystified by what I perceived to be an odd police term, my quizzical look must have betrayed my puzzlement.

"That's what we call this guy because he wears hiking boots that have that waffle pattern on the sole. He's been scaring a lot of people lately and I guess this was his welcome visit for you guys. He had to see what the new people in town were like."

To further lull our fears he added, "So far he's been harmless, but you'd better keep your doors locked just in case."

With that, the two officers took their leave saying that a patrol car would keep on the lookout and check the area several times during the night.

Somehow, I didn't feel reassured.

Sleeping that night seemed an impossible proposition in spite of the pistol constantly in my sight. I had everybody sleep in the same room, and was grateful for the early sunrise of the late Alaskan summer.

It took another week before the telephone company could work us into their schedule for a hook up.

Many times I asked myself: had we been crazy to leave the safety of the wilds for the dangers of civilization?

∂∘ CHAPTER 3 ✄

MAYDAY IN AUGUST

"Tuesday was the second bad day for Mr. Bob Norberg..." began the article in the Fairbanks Daily News that first week in August.

Back up in Fairbanks, Bob was having his own bad time. The article was referring to his less-than-successful attempt at logging some flying time towards his pilot's license.

It started innocently enough. Having flown into Fairbanks from Tanana where the plane had been sitting for a while, Bob found that he needed to use the facilities. He taxied up to the fuel station. Seeing the very young attendant standing around, told him to keep an eye on the plane until he came back to fuel up. He figured that despite his extreme youth, the kid could handle the guarding. Gassing up his baby however, well, that took someone more senior.

Unfortunately, the attendant was not about to have his talents ignored. By the time Bob returned, the tanks had been topped off by the now smugly smiling youth. There was nothing to do but to feel the gas caps to make sure they were tight. Given that these were above the wing, unless you were about eight feet tall, this maneuver was necessarily performed by Braille.

* * *

"Eight-Three-One-Eight Victor ready to roll," announced the pilot to the tower as he taxied out onto the airstrip.

It was a beautiful day for flying. Small white clouds scudded along a brilliant blue sky propelled by a very light, easterly wind.

One or two knots probably. Visibility was infinite as it's prone to be on the last frontier, especially during the summer months. The trees were beginning to turn gold, and there was plenty of water in the rivers and streams.

As Bob took care of the preliminaries, advising the tower that his flight plan called for a return in the late afternoon, he turned into what little wind there was, eagerly awaiting the peaceful exhilaration of the flight.

Fairbanks fell away as his red and white striped Citabria strained in its ascent and he marveled for the hundredth time at the distant scenery below.

Preparation for the final pilot's test required him to do some steep "S" curves. He decided that now would be a good time to get in some practice on those maneuvers.

He saw a power line where the spruce trees had been cut down so that it looked like a giant snake cutting a straight swath up the dense hillsides.

He would use this as a reference point.

Swooping from side to side of the power line, getting into the exercise, Bob was completely unprepared for what happened next.

A cough. Not his; the plane's.

And then another. And yet another.

Then silence.

Total silence.

His heart made the short journey to his mouth, but his brain had been channeled by practice to immediately run down the possibilities.

It was an easy conclusion. The engine had stopped because it wasn't getting any gas. (A good clue was the gas gauge reading "E.") The propeller was still; the wind rushed past the plane making an eerie whistling sound.

There was another sound, too.

A very loud heartbeat.

After easing the stick and coaxing the rudder pedals, he pulled the switch to the second gas tank—to no avail. It was on "E" too.

Maybe there was something caught in the carburetor.

Sweat breaking out, Bob madly worked the primer

back and forth to try to inject a spurt of fuel into the engine, hoping that whatever was caught in the line or the carburetor would be dislodged and the engine would catch.

All the time asking himself how he could be out of gas when the tanks had just been topped off, his mind automatically went over what he had learned to do in a case like this.

He set up the proper ratio for glide speed and realized that, at 1700 feet of altitude, there was no way he could glide the five or so miles back to Fairbanks Airport.

He had to find something nearby.

Looking down, he could see this was much easier said than done. There was nothing but a carpet of spongy, tangled tundra beneath.

"Mayday! Mayday! Eight three one eight Victor going down five miles southwest of Fairbanks International."

It was like acting in a B movie. Maybe a C, if there was such a thing.

"One eight Victor. We're trying to pick you up on the radar. Give us your vectors."

Bob did so.

"One eight Victor, is there anything you want us to do?"

Bob knew that what they really meant was: "Whom do you want us to notify?"

In a brash attempt at humor, he retorted, "Yeah. Move the airport underneath me!"

Before they had a chance to reply—probably a good thing—he continued, "By the way, I'm going to be busy for the next few minutes. Out."

One can only imagine what they were thinking.

His mind on survival tactics, Bob knew what he needed to be thinking. He hit the starter button to shut off all the electricity. The same for the fuel switch, and the master switches.

Below, as far as he could strain his eyes, he could see the glint of sunlight reflected by the billions of little puddles of water riddling the mossy tundra.

A landing place guaranteed to grab your wheels and flip you over.

He remembered the story he had heard about the World War II Japanese fighter pilot whose oil gauge line had been severed by a bullet so that it read empty and he thought he was out of oil. When he tried to land his Zero on Attu Island before his engine had a chance to seize, he lowered the wheels and the tundra grabbed them, flipping him over and snapping his neck.

Thus, the pilot had made an unwitting contribution to the US by making available the design of his plane. The Americans immediately used the design, improved on it, and produced their own new fighter planes.

Ah, American ingenuity.

Bob was not eager to replicate that unfortunate pilot's landing.

But where could he go...and quickly? Everywhere the water twinkled and the tundra threatened. Except...

Except for a tiny gray sandbar shaped like a dog's

leg, jutting into a little tiny creek. Well, it looked little and harmless from that height.

Bob adjusted the trajectory to line up with the sandbar. The spiky sixty-foot spruce trees at one end made the gliding to a smooth and easy stop very tricky.

If he'd had time, Bob would have been very proud of the way he slipped the plane down to the sandbar, textbook fashion, skimming the treetops, and landing lightly, curving around the dogleg to an almost perfect stop.

Well, it would have been perfect if not for a muddy puddle at the very end of the gravel.

As the wheels locked, and grass and brush flew by, the plane slowed down. It was time for a well-earned sigh of relief.

Almost.

There was the small matter of the mud puddle at the end of the sandbar. A little muddy dip, nothing more. The front wheels sank into the mud, bringing the ride to an abrupt end. But the tail kept on going. It flipped up and over the nose very gently, almost in slow motion. The fuselage finally came to rest upside down, tail resting on some brush.

Inside, still strapped in, Bob feared fire even though he knew in the back of his mind that there supposedly wasn't any fuel. In his hurry to escape, and forgetting he was suspended upside down, he popped his seatbelt and promptly fell on his head crashing to the ceiling of the plane, in a jumbled tangle of arms and legs.

Fumbling for the door, and banging his elbows and shins on the dashboard, not being able to see because of the dust and bits of grit that had fallen to the ceiling from the floor, he finally opened the door and breast stroked his way along the underside of the wing that was now on top.

Reaching the end of the wing, he rolled to the ground and sprinted away from the plane. At about fifty feet, he stopped, turned around, half expecting the plane to burst into flames.

In silence except for the wind and water, he waited. Then, figuring that there really weren't any gas or fumes left in the plane, he went back towards it to get his survival kit and to assess the damage.

He found it to be minimal: just a little bend in the prop.

Not bad, considering. Resigned to wait, it wasn't too long before Bob heard a helicopter's rotors. It was a Bell 47, its big glass bubble glinting in the sun.

As it landed, Bob walked toward it, ready to greet the pilot.

But, instead of the pilot, holding his Smokey the Bear hat in his hand and a stern look on his face, a state trooper piled out.

"Oh no, you're not going to give me a ticket are you?"

At this rate, anything was possible. In his addled state, Bob was thinking that he had destroyed some of the state's shrubbery and he wasn't exactly parked legally.

The trooper good-naturedly calmed his fears, telling him that he had just been going off duty when the tower had alerted him that first aid might be needed in a rescue, so he had jumped into the helicopter to see if he could help.

The ride back to Fairbanks was uneventful. Bob went right over to see Phil, his instructor.

That night, they both tried to figure out how his gas had disappeared. They came to the conclusion that the gasoline attendant had probably dropped the gas cap, jarring loose the gasket. He hadn't seen it fall out, and, lacking experience, hadn't checked. Later, during the maneuvers Bob had practiced—including deep turns where the wings would dip significantly—with no gasket to block its exit, the gas had siphoned its way out thanks to the negative air pressure on the surface of the wing.

The next day, Tuesday, Bob and Phil borrowed another Citabria, this one on floats, in order to land on the creek next to the downed plane.

The long range plan was to flip the plane back over, to empty everything out to make it lighter, to gas it, to brush out part of the sandbar to make a better takeoff strip, and, finally, to fly it out.

The short-range plan was to fly out and take a good look at the crash site to take inventory of the situation.

As they flew back to the not-exactly-in-mint-condition plane, Bob was full of confidence that his troubles would soon end. Phil had several hundred hours of flying on floats. He was a skilled pilot who knew all of the particular aspects of Alaskan flying. This was a day in the park for him.

As they approached the site, they had to quickly drop below the trees and actually had to fly below the bank level since the creek level was even lower.

The creek was extremely narrow; there were only about ten feet of clearance at each wing tip.

They came in too fast and on an angle. The creek was amazingly swift. One float hit the water with such impact that the plane ricocheted sideways into the bank. The plane bounced and the nose tipped into the rushing water. The struts tore loose, the frame and wing bent.

Phil yelled to Bob to get out and started to scramble out himself only to find that Bob was already out, balanced on a float, extending a helping hand. How he had climbed out of the back seat over Phil's shoulder and out the door remains a mystery to this day. It was possibly due to his having practiced quick exits before.

The float Bob was standing on was completely bent upward, smashed against the side of the fuselage.

Once out of the plane, and half submerged in the creek, they wrestled the plane to a spot on the bank where it wouldn't be dislodged. After catching their breath they managed to get in a "Mayday-need-assistance" to the tower. Upon hearing the location for the second time in as many days, the controller was understandably incredulous.

"What? Is this for real?" he asked, departing from the usual droning "tower" terminology.

As in a bad case of déjà vu, Bob found himself

waiting, once again, for rescue.

After about twenty minutes, they heard an enormously loud "whop-whop" of rotor blades. It was so loud they couldn't imagine what was coming. When it finally came into view they recognized a Sikorsky Sky-Crane, the biggest helicopter on the free world at that time. (Only the Soviet Union had one a little bigger.)

In Bob's opinion, this might have been a case of over-kill, but he was nevertheless very much in awe of the flying monster.

His awe soon turned to horror however, as the prop wash of the hovering 'copter made the damaged planes on the ground bounce up and down with incredible force. The wash also kicked up rocks and gravel boulders.

Panicked, both maroonees started yelling and gesturing for the pilot to move away.

When they resorted to throwing rocks at the helicopter, the pilot finally got the message and moved off toward the other end of the gravel bar.

Not managing very well to hide his anger, Bob did calm down long enough to find out why this machine had come to the rescue this time.

The story was that the crane had been heading to Fort Richardson air force base when the mayday had come over the radio. The crew figured they might as well be the ones to go on the rescue mission.

Once more Bob sat in a helicopter heading back to Fairbanks. This time he was farther behind than before because now there were two planes to salvage. It was all beginning to take on the proportions of an even worse script than before.

As he sat with earphones on against the deafening engine noise, he couldn't help feeling guilty over the damage to the floatplane, and he was having real trouble trying to figure out how to get out of this mess.

Insult was added to injury as, when he walked into Fairbanks airport having just gotten out of the helicopter whose noise had alerted everyone within miles, he ran right into the trooper who had rescued him the first time.

The trooper, who had seen Bob get out of the sky-crane, made some inquiry as to the new problem. Something diplomatic and tactful like, "Now what did you do?"

Bob begged off, insisting that he was merely the passenger in this second installment of the fiasco.

One can only surmise what the trooper thought, as he pursed his lips and shook his head.

The real question now was what the next move was going to be.

A few phone calls later they learned that the owner of the floatplane had insurance to cover rescuing the plane. The rescue would involve yet another helicopter outfitted with a special sling made to lift planes. Bob, however, had no such insurance, so the bill would be his responsibility. No one is eager to insure a novice.

Equipped with miles of rope, Bob and Phil made the journey back to the gravel bar seated in the third helicopter of the last twenty-four hours.

The idea was to tie the airplanes to the sling that the helicopter would gently lift and fly back to Fairbanks.

The problem is that as soon as the airplane gets into the air, it wants to fly on its own. Bob and Phil had to sign a waiver that if the plane began to sway, the helicopter pilot would "pickle" them. That meant he would press a button with his thumb that would release the rope and drop them right back to the ground. Otherwise, if the plane started swaying too violently, there would be a much worse kind of accident.

Having no choice but to sign, Bob did so.

In order to make the floatplane as un-aerodynamic as possible, they tied brush to the top of the wings to prevent lift, and a log to the tail for added drag. That would make the plane more stable in the air.

With bated breath, they watched as the floatplane was slowly lifted off the ground. It swung a little, but then calmed down as the helicopter hovered over head. Then, still very slowly, it made its way east. Soon it was lost in the distance.

They started work on Bob's Citabria that was still upside down, tail resting on the bushes. They used one of the ropes to truss it like a chicken to create drag.

When the helicopter returned, someone suggested using the helicopter to gently tip the plane back over. The loadmaster said they should tie a rope from the helicopter to the little handle by the tail of the plane.

The helicopter would rise just a few feet, tipping the plane gently back upright.

Bob was not convinced. He knew the handle would not sustain the entire weight of the airplane if the helicopter should pull it off the ground. He expressed his fears but was told not to worry. The helicopter would not pull it all the way off the ground.

So, the loadmaster crawled back into the helicopter and lay on his belly to judge the distances involved in just tipping the plane back over.

Someone must have gotten the signals crossed. All of a sudden, the plane was jerked up into the air about ten feet. The handle snapped right off and the plane landed on its wingtip, crumpling it.

With the weight of two days of frustration pressurizing him, Bob went a little crazy. As the helicopter crew landed to further discuss the situation, they were met by a maniac with his hand on his holstered .44 pistol yelling something to the effect that they might well have survived Viet Nam but they were going to die at home. He was going to "pickle" his gun. He let them know he was paying good money for this operation and now it had just become more expensive.

It took a while to calm him down. They finally managed to tie the plane to the helicopter and slowly lift it back to the airport.

Later, the crew demonstrated enough bravery to go back and pick up the two stranded pilots, one of whom was still seething.

Luckily there was too much engine noise for

conversation.

Insult and injury were still not over, however. The Federal Aviation Agency sent out two agents to check the damage on the planes. In order to get a better view of the framework, one of the agents took out his pocketknife and slit the fabric we had spent so many hours repainting. Bob exploded again. Phil chimed in that the rules did not specify going that far for an inspection. Not realizing he might be risking his life, the agent simply shrugged and went over to the other side, his knife still in hand. He was just about to make another cut when he must have gotten a funny feeling and stopped. Someone was standing much too close, right behind him.

I guess he got a good look at Bob's face this time because in less than a minute, he was scooting along the tarmac back to his office, never to return.

The saga of the "little Citabria-that-couldn't" continued much later when a friend tied it to a pick-up truck to haul it the thousand miles from Fairbanks to Homer for us. The truck ride damaged it even more, and it sat morosely in the yard for a long time.

One day, I looked out the kitchen window to see a cow moose walking across the wings stored on the ground. In spite of all the insult, I'm convinced it will soar again.

❧ CHAPTER 4 ❧

ON FROZEN GROUND

By the time school began, our perennial constant, we had fallen into a routine. Our phone was finally hooked up, Geoff was registered for the afternoon session of Kindergarten, and Bob had begun his new job at the junior high school.

Our house was close to everything, but even though it was "in town," we had a panoramic view of Kachemak Bay complete with glaciers. During the coldest part of the winter, (very mild compared to our previous ones) the Alaskan flavor of moose in the back yard was still reality. One, in particular, continued to walk all over the snow-covered airplane wing that was still outside.

Because the weather was so mild, never even approaching zero and barely going below freezing most of the time, we made the most of exploring the area. One of our favorite weekend excursions was driving to the end of the "Homer Spit," a six-mile long strip of land extending into the bay, to have lunch at the "Land's End" restaurant and walk the extensive beach. The "spit" had once boasted a fairly large wooded area on the eastside, but the 1964 earthquake had caused the whole area to sink six feet. All that was left was a stringy copse of dead trunks, vestiges of sizeable spruce trees. At high tide, only the road with a few feet of land to each side rose above the water level. At extra-high tides during any kind of storm, the road became impassable, stranding anyone who had the misfortune to be caught at the far end of the Spit.

On the way back home during those weekend excursions, we would pass by a certain area of town that consisted of a loop road that didn't quite make an entire loop. On one end of the loop, the houses faced directly south with a view of the bay and spit. On the other end, the view was westerly. From there, you could look out to sea at Mt. Augustine, an active volcano sixty miles away. There was a gravel and sand beach, tall spruce trees, a tidal slough around the corner and plenty of privacy.

We fell in love with one of the lots there, thinking it would be a perfect place to build our house. The problem was that we didn't even know who owned the land, nor if it was even for sale.

After some considerable research, we were able to find out that the owners of the land lived in Texas. It didn't take long to correspond with them and buy the acre on the beach.

This began the era of house building, which was

for most people in those parts, an era without end. Although we'd had experience of building small structures from the fish wheel to the rec room we had added to the trailer in Tanana, and Bob had spent some of his youth working on construction sites, we were basically ignorant in the field.

We did realize that a basic aspect to house building is to work from bottom up, but as time went on, even though we tried to adhere to that principle, we found ourselves veering from it.

It all started when we hired someone to dig the foundation. He came on schedule with his caterpillar and began the digging. Then the fishing bug hit. The next day he was off on a boat. From the spot where our living room window was projected to be, we watched it disappear over the horizon.

There was nothing to do but wait until he came back.

Meanwhile, the weather turned unseasonably cold. The ground froze. When our digger came back from a two-week absence, he said we'd have to loosen the ground a bit.

"How do you do that?" we innocently, but warily, wanted to know.

"Dynamite" he answered matter-of-factly, as if to say, "What other way is there, dummy?"

What did we know...?

A few sticks and charges and the deed was done. The ground was "loose."

He finished digging the foundation.

313

We were now three weeks behind schedule. This meant working in much colder temperatures. In order to combat the cold, we set up a huge visqueen tent over the entire foundation.

Visqueen was a survival material; kind of like the plastic wrap you use in the kitchen to store leftovers, except that it's extremely strong and comes on huge rolls. Many people lived in it, under it, or on it for years. It kept out wind, rain, snow and small predators. There were many temporary shelters made of it—temporary-forever, in some cases.

Under the tent, we had two or three huge and powerful space heaters to try to keep the workers and the building materials from freezing. At night the lights underneath the plastic made the entire site look like a mysterious archeological dig on a distant planet.

Everything was fine until the wind picked up and blew the tent apart. When that happened, it took hours to set up again.

The next item on the agenda was pouring the footers. It was pretty difficult to get the cement truck into the property because we didn't want to sacrifice any of the trees. They had to get an extra long chute to get the cement into the footer forms.

The footers finally poured, we moved on to the next step.

Because we wanted to be able to enjoy the view, we decided to put in a crawl space basement and build the first floor completely above ground with big windows facing the beach. If we were able to later on, we'd add a second story.

Everything was pretty much going as planned until the day someone noticed that the beachside footers, the ones put in the dynamited area, were sinking. The dynamite had fractured the ground so much that its consistency was now too "loose." The weight and the settling of the building had caused the footers to sink. By contrast, the first footers, the ones poured on the "unloosened" ground, were fine.

"Now what do we do?"

"Oh, that's simple," we were told. "All we do is rest the beachside of the house on a bunch of fifty gallon drums, wait for spring, and then re-pour the bad footers."

Totally ignorant in these matters, we could only agree. We spent our first winter in our half-built house, half on firm ground, and half on fifty-gallon drums. These drums, along with the aforementioned visqueen, were an important factor in Alaskan architecture. Uses for the drums could fill volumes. Our example was only one of the many.

As we thought about the redo work that lay ahead of us, someone had the bright idea to make the crawl space into a daylight basement so that the view could be seen from down there too.

With some trepidation we inquired as to how that might be accomplished and what it would involve.

"Oh, not too much," came the answer. "We'll hire the Russians to jack up the house and put it up on pilings while we re-do the footers and build the basement walls."

As an afterthought the speaker added, "Of course, you won't have any water or sewer for a while because we'll have to disconnect the pipes. Oh, and you'll need a big ladder to get in and out of the house because we can't build the stairs until the basement walls are up."

What could we say? Something told me normal house building didn't happen like this, but who were we to question the experts?

So, we resigned ourselves to using the locker rooms at school for showers and laundry. The toilet situation had to be dealt with as well. Serious business had to be conducted at school. The non-serious was taken care of at home, in the great outdoors.

The Russians were coming.

About forty miles up the highway and down through winding dirt roads from Homer was the little settlement of Nikolaevsk. It was a little village settled by people originally from Russia. Most made their living by fishing and construction. Although the older generation really stuck to themselves and preserved the "old ways," the younger generation was becoming quite Americanized. As a group, they seemed particularly well versed in some of the more odd building problems. Hence, their impending visit to our building site.

The water and sewer lines were cut. The Russians pulled out their jacks, shims, and hundreds of pieces of cribbing material.

I was apprehensive about this whole thing so I decided not to watch. Instead I stayed in the house with the kids. That probably ended up being much more nerve wracking. As the house was jacked up, it creaked, snapped and tottered at odd angles. It swayed enough to make you think you were at sea. I expected everything to come toppling down at any moment. Since I couldn't keep busy with laundry, dishes or a soothing bath, and I was way too keyed up to read, there was nothing to do but grit my teeth and hope nobody would be hurt or crushed by a falling house.

After long hours, the house stood, almost still, completely supported on fifteen or so skinny little towers of cribbing material.

As they worked on re-pouring the bad footers, and building the block walls of the basement, we became quite proficient at climbing up and down the ladder (that spanned a twenty-foot deep ditch) to get in and out of the house, sometimes laden with grocery bags etc. Even Stephanie, who had just turned two, could crawl up and down quite well by herself. She had no idea it wasn't normal to enter your own house that way.

It did keep visitors away though. No one liked the idea of the ladder, and most were afraid they'd get seasick once they did get inside the house.

The absence of a working toilet was a deterrent as well.

With time, our odd living conditions became routine. Besides the constant struggle with the cold; using the large noisy space heaters in the construction area underneath the house, making do without plumbing and water, there was only one occasion of real panic.

317

We realized, by this time, that living on the beach means a whole bunch of wind. From one in the afternoon, it blows relentlessly until six or seven. Except in the cases of storms, it usually calms down in the evening. On rainy, misty days, it doesn't even blow at all.

One of the nights while we were still perched on our "towers," the wind picked up uncharacteristically, late in the evening. It got progressively worse, and by the time we went to bed, we were swaying considerably. Tired as we were, we dozed off only to be awakened in the middle of the night by a particularly loud and violent gust.

The house was swaying and creaking much more seriously than before. We looked toward each other in the darkness, wondering who would express fear first.

The next gust had us both on our feet, hurriedly throwing on our jackets and boots. Bob grabbed great lengths of rope from our building junk-pile and we opened the door to go down the ladder.

It wasn't there. There was just a great gaping hole of darkness.

The wind wrenched the door from our grasp and banged it against the some metal shelves that lined the wall.

We had no choice but to anchor one of the pieces of rope to the shelves. Bob climbed down the rope, the wind whipping him against the side of the house.

He looked around in the darkness and found the ladder. It had fallen in the ditch that encircled the house. He slid down the mud and retrieved it. Using it to climb out of the ditch, he then propped it against the house for me to climb down. I threw all the rope to the ground and slid down the slippery ladder.

Somehow, in the dark, we were going to tie this house down so that it didn't slide off the cribbing.

Using his best boy scout and sailor knots, Bob tied several of the lengths of rope together.

The wind and rain whipping around us, we each made our way to opposite sides of the house. Bob coiled a length of rope and, keeping a grip on one end, he threw the rest of it over the top of the house. On the other side, more hearing it slap the side of the house than seeing it, I grabbed what came over. I then fed that end under the house, in between the piles of cribbing, so that by the time Bob had a hold of that end of the rope again, we had a giant loop around the entire building. He then tied another knot, a very substantial one, and tied the leftover length to one of the huge spruce trees, making sure there was plenty of tension.

We repeated the same procedure once more, in a different spot and used a different tree. We now had two huge loops around the house, tied to two trees.

It probably didn't really help a bit. If the wind could blow the house down, our measly rope trick probably wouldn't help much.

But, we felt better about it non-the-less.

Thoroughly soaked and frozen, we climbed back inside and checked on the kids. Incredibly, they were still fast asleep, not knowing that they were supposed to be scared to death.

319

As we got ready to go back to bed, I looked out the bedroom window.

Somehow, the clouds must have parted in one spot, because I caught a flash of moonlight on the giant buoy that Bob had tied to a tree branch for the kids to use as a swing. It was bouncing and swinging violently.

It reminded me of years ago in Togiak. During a quiet moment in class, on a windy day in spring, one of the kids looked out on the playground at the swings moving on their own, exclaiming as she pointed outside, "Look, look, teacher. The wind is playing!"

And so it had. From the tundra of Togiak, to the mighty Yukon River, to the wide beaches of the Kenai Peninsula, it had buffeted us, wherever we had been.

❧ EPILOGUE ❧

The sky is still mostly dark in the calm pre-dawn hours of a fall morning. To the east, reflected on the far-off snowy peaks, streaks of pink between great striations of clouds left over from a recent storm promise a bright sunrise still an hour away. The dawn imposes a deep stillness on the beach; the water, silent, barely ebbing, leaves a frothy line of foam scalloping the edge of the sand.

Down by the low-tide mark, in an area full of rocks and boulders, a military six-by-six flatbed truck tears the silence as it rumbles in fits and starts over the uneven ground. Its axles, reminiscent of the legs of a caterpillar, lever up and down to gain clearance. Whining, the engine strains to gain momentum. The carriage squeaks and scrapes as it absorbs the shock of bottoming out between boulders.

The engine stops. The silence returns enveloping five small figures as they pile out of the truck. The two taller figures walk purposefully in opposite directions,

321

intent on finding something among the gravel and rocks. One of the figures carries a long crowbar.

Finding a smooth sandy spot, the three smaller figures create wild circles as they chase each other and squeal with glee.

Then, by some unspoken signal, they bend down to pick up a large but deceptively light black rock.

"I found one, Mom," yells one of the small figures.

"Me, too, and it's really big. Look!" yells the smallest.

"Okay, you guys, put them by the truck and look for some more."

Grunting with effort, the children lumber over to the truck with their find.

By the time the sun has erased all vestiges of darkness, the flatbed is piled high with several hundred pounds of great black chunks.

"Okay. That should hold us until the next storm. The tide's coming back up, anyway. Who wants to drive home?"

There's a chorus "Me! Me!" as everyone piles back into the truck.

In spite of not being able to reach the pedals, each driver gets a turn at the wheel of the truck as it rumbles back down the beach to head for home.

Thanks to nature's bounty, there's now several months' worth of free heating fuel in the truck. Last night's storm has ripped the chunks of coal from the large vein of it in the cliffs and the tide has spread it all out on the beach. Pretty soon, the beach will be dotted with others who have come for the same thing. So, while the rest of the world is watching Saturday morning cartoons, hundreds of pounds of coal have been collected by the whole family to put in the furnace at home.

Sound primitive?

People have remarked with loud incredulity, "I can't believe you actually made the kids pick coal to heat the house with... It sounds so...so... well... basic..."

Well, maybe so. But it has its value. The children know what it takes to accomplish something, and they have never shied away from putting effort into what they do.

Our story ends here.

Except for some slightly-out-of-the-ordinary things, our lives in the house by the sea, took on the appearance of a completely normal family. Sure, we sometimes did things a little differently: our kids almost never sat in front of the television. On Saturday mornings, they were either helping, building, or going to sports practice. But they also enjoyed the benefits of their environment. They spent hours playing on the beach accompanied by Dusty, our golden retriever. They'd fish in the slough or collect tadpoles in the small rain ponds. They'd climb trees or build driftwood forts. Beach picnics soon numbered in the hundreds. Idleness was never in their vocabulary.

* * *

When I add up the positives and the negatives of our lives, and mix them with a healthy dose of humor, I come up with a pretty good concoction. Like the wind, Fate plays with us. It warms or cools, pushes and pulls, and always gives us challenges by which to measure our mettle.

 THE END

YOU CAN'T WALLPAPER MY IGLOO

ABOUT THE AUTHOR

⌘

Since her birth and childhood education in Brussels, Belgium, Katherine Norberg has spent most of her life teaching and writing about children of all ages and backgrounds. Seventeen of her years were spent surviving the wilderness of Alaska in and out of the classroom. The great contrast of her recent years in Los Angeles has prompted her to reminisce about her experiences in the North, where she and her husband began their lives together. A healthy sense of humor, and a desire to be self-sufficient kept them both going when engines broke down, pipes froze, Christmas presents didn't arrive, and students had their own ideas about education.

Having published several articles in local papers and magazines, Katherine decided to indulge her love of writing by putting everything together in *You Can't Wallpaper My Igloo* hoping to preserve long lasting images of a rapidly vanishing and unique way of life.

The author now splits her time between Alaska and California, where she visits friends and family.

34341405R00187

Made in the USA
Middletown, DE
18 August 2016